T0276995

# THIS MOUTH IS MINE

First published by Charco Press 2024
Charco Press Ltd., Office 59, 44-46 Morningside Road, Edinburgh
EH10 4BF

Copyright © Yásnaya Elena A. Gil, 2020
First published in Spanish as
*Ää: manifiestos sobre la diversidad lingüística* (Mexico City: Almadía)
English translation copyright © Ellen Jones, 2024

The rights of Yásnaya Elena A. Gil to be identified as the author of this
work and of Ellen Jones to be identified as the translator of this work
have been asserted by them in accordance with the Copyright, Designs
and Patents Act 1988.

All rights reserved. This book is copyright material and must not be
copied, reproduced, transferred, distributed, leased, licensed or publicly
performed or used in any way except as specifically permitted in
writing by the publisher, as allowed under the terms and conditions
under which it was purchased or as strictly permitted by the applicable
copyright law. Any unauthorised distribution or use of this text may be
a direct infringement of the author's and publisher's rights, and those
responsible may be liable in law accordingly.

A CIP catalogue record for this book is available
from the British Library.

ISBN: 9781913867966
e-book: 9781913867973

www.charcopress.com

Edited by Fionn Petch
Cover designed by Pablo Font
Typeset by Laura Jones-Rivera
Proofread by Fiona Mackintosh

Yásnaya Elena A. Gil

# THIS MOUTH IS MINE

Translated by
Ellen Jones

Originally compiled by
Ana Aguilar Guevara, Julia Bravo Varela, Gustavo
Ogarrio Badillo and Valentina Quaresma Rodríguez

CHARCO PRESS

# CONTENTS

## Part III: WHAT SHALL WE CALL HER, MATARILERILERÓ?

*Amuum tu'uk joojt Nan Len: ka'ookyë'm ja*
*m'ää m'ayuujk tsyuj.*
*Pojën jatëkoojk nnaypääjtën, mami.*

This book, like many things in life made slowly and with love, would not have been possible without the support of several key figures. We are grateful to the Research Coordinators at the Faculty of Philosophy and Letters at the National Autonomous University of Mexico for their full support through the PIFFYL 2016024 project, 'Paradigmas del estudio y divulgación de la diversidad lingüística'. We'd also like to affectionately thank César Alejandro Paredes Rendón and Ana Laura Arrieta Zamudio for their collaboration in the research process. We also thank the people at Almadía, the original publishers, for sharing our enthusiasm for this project and for seeing it through to fruition with such commitment. Finally, thank you to Federico Navarrete Linares for his magnificent prologue.

**Ana Aguilar Guevara**
**Julia Bravo Varela**
**Gustavo Ogarrio Badillo**
**Valentina Quaresma Rodríguez**

# PROLOGUE

## Federico Navarrete Linares

Reading the essays by Yásnaya Aguilar collected in this volume, originally published in the magazine *Este País* between 2011 and 2015, alongside the many social media posts that accompanied and enriched them during that period, is a pleasure I recommend wholeheartedly to readers. For me it is an honour to write this prologue, which is a continuation of the conversations, both public and private, Yásnaya and I had over the course of half a decade, from 2014, when I invited her to speak to participants in a seminar titled 'Pensando contra el racismo' (Thinking Against Racism) at the National Autonomous University of Mexico (UNAM), to 2019, when she asked my opinion on her speech – the first ever to be delivered in Ayuujk or Mixe – to the Colegio Nacional, through many other pleasurable occasions along the way. All these occasions have confirmed to me her exceptional communication skills, the originality of her ideas, her mastery of the most varied styles of discourse, from X (formerly Twitter) and Facebook posts, by way of the university Spanish of academic events, to the elevated

Ayuujk euphemisms used in the community assembly of San Pedro and San Pablo Ayutla in the Mixe region of Oaxaca, her home town and place of residence both out of choice and as the result of her vocation. In all these different environments, Yas, as she is known among friends, has shown her intelligence, her commitment and, above all, her modesty, honesty, and the profound sincerity of her voice and her thinking.

This edited collection, put together by colleagues and friends Ana Aguilar Guevara, Julia Bravo Varela, Gustavo Ogarrio Badillo and Valentina Quaresma Rodríguez, allows us to continue her personal, political and intellectual journey, from when she was just starting out as a public writer, to the present day, when she has emerged as one of contemporary Mexico's most original and interesting thinkers. And although the central theme of these pieces is languages and their uses, the author's questions and reflections go beyond that, tackling key problems in the history and life of our country and especially of its Indigenous communities. These articles, enriched with the freshness of everyday life, with lived anecdotes, with personal experience, with shared struggles and conversations, show us beyond all doubt that linguistics is political, that the relationship between Spanish and the at least 365 other languages in Mexico, belonging to sixty-eight linguistic systems, is a key part of the history of the building of the nation state and of the racism and violence that accompanied it.

In terms of its own use of language, this collection gives a fairly unusual perspective on our literary landscape: a new, fresh female voice, a native speaker of Ayuujk who uses Spanish as a tool for communication and questioning, rather than as a language of prestige. The same could be said of linguistics and its conceptual tools, which Yásnaya uses deftly, integrating them skilfully

2

and productively into a discourse that never pretends to be academic, but rather is accessible and appealing to all kinds of readers.

In Spanish, Yásnaya's style is always direct and honest, full of informal expression and indifferent to the stylistic pretensions of the 'cultured' elite. She writes it as she learned it, from below, like the millions of other Mexicans who first learned a different mother tongue and were then confronted with the dominant language at school, in the media, in public life, in political life, and had to absorb it one misstep at a time, amid restrictions and threats; who were forced to do so, basically, because there was no alternative. This collection is an effective, precise denunciation of the abuse that has accompanied the forced 'Hispanicisation' of Indigenous language speakers, from the suffering of pupils in rural boarding schools to the daily contempt directed at them by their 'bilingual' teachers. It also narrates the author's own experiences, in Mexico City and other social environments, when confronted with prejudice – as finely tuned as it was irrational – against Indigenous languages and their speakers.

And yet Yásnaya demonstrates and celebrates her love of Spanish, born during her days as a primary school pupil when she began, before actually learning the language, to decipher the alphabet, shaping her mouth around its still unfamiliar sounds until they resounded in her ears, sounds charged with meanings that were to her unimaginable and all the more appealing for it. She also tells us of her first journeys to cities around the country, where she assumed bilingual schools would teach Spanish and the local Indigenous language, such as Nahuatl in Mexico City, but was soon disappointed to discover that they taught English, thus realising that in this country, as in its schools, being bilingual in European languages

3

is not the same as being bilingual in Ayuujk or Ñahñu. Throughout these texts, which are as entertaining as they are refreshing, it is clear that Yásnaya has been able to look beyond the impositions and the violence, driven by her deep passion for languages, for linguistics, for literature, for going beyond the confines of her native Ayuujk and her acquired Spanish to learn both about the world's most widely spoken languages, such as Russian, and also about the innumerable Indigenous languages around the globe that find themselves marginalised, threatened and sometimes on the verge of disappearing.

I should add here that even a speaker and writer as talented as Yásnaya occasionally feels intimidated, though not by the Spanish of this country's dull, authoritarian academics, but rather by the subtleties of vocabulary and the 'ceremonial' style of Mixe spoken in her native Ayutla, the elevated and elegant language of the assemblies that embody the community's thinking and its political traditions. My conversations over the years with her and other friends, both Mixe and non-Mixe, have shown me the conceptual depth that underlies this form of governance, which Yas, in her own subversive way, has compared to anarchism.

In her unpretentious use of Mexico's everyday variety of Spanish we can see the constant generosity of her style, her humour and her sincerity, which allow her to build a defence – as passionate as it is logical, as rigorous as it is entertaining – of the value of Indigenous languages, of cultural plurality, and of the vitality of our original peoples' traditions. This clarity gives greater strength, too, to her denunciations of linguistic discrimination, of contempt for Indigenous languages and of the arrogance of those who defend Spanish as the national language. Written over the course of a decade, this book is also an intimate, honest diary that allows us to

4

follow the author's trajectory as an activist for linguistic diversity, through confusions and mysteries, reflections and conversations, mistakes and disappointments as well as small achievements and wins, both in her community and beyond, that have opened up a space for Ayuujk and other Indigenous languages.

This defence turns out to be doubly effective and surprising because Yásnaya argues it without resorting to the essentialist definitions so prevalent in academic and political publications, such as the insistence on the continuity of Indigenous cultures and cosmovisions, in the irrevocable unity of 'deep Mexico' or the authenticity of Mesoamerican ways of life as the 'roots' of our identity. The intellectual honesty and real modesty of her thinking prevents her from constructing an idealised or simplified vision of Indigenous cultural and linguistic realities; rather, she shows them in all their diversity and with all their contradictions. This plural, nuanced vision is built on real, lived experience, of her own and shared knowledge, of conversations with people of every kind. To define her relationship with the Ayuujk language, for example, she begins with her *communalect*, which is to say the variety spoken in Ayutla, her hometown, before tackling varieties in neighbouring communities and then finally discussing the language as a whole. In her intimate and honest description of this plural reality, she makes sure to point out the gaps in her own knowledge, the mistakes she has made and failures she has had as an activist and the ideas and support she has received from comrades in arms, beginning with the other members of COLMIX, a research collective dedicated to reflecting on the Mixe region and Oaxaca's Indigenous communities.

One of the most interesting novelties of Yásnaya's thinking, developed throughout these essays, is her essentially political conceptualisation of the identity of

5

Indigenous communities. She argues and demonstrates that what this great diversity of peoples, communities and groups have in common is not a way of life or a culture, for those are as different as the languages they speak, but rather a specific and particular relationship with the state and with the internal colonialism and racism they have suffered. Indigenous communities are not the roots of the Mexican nation but rather its effective negation: they are nations that existed before it was formed, that did not participate in its definition – driven by the criollo and mestizo elites – and which have been in large part its historical victims; what is more, today they maintain types of community and regional organisation that are independent or at least autonomous from the state. Their stance is informed at once by anarchist ideology and by the communalist tradition of Mixe thinkers, a diversity of influences and affinities that demonstrate the cultural and political openness of the Indigenous 'resistance' practiced by Yásnaya and a new generation of Indigenous thinkers. As this book repeatedly shows, there is just as much space here for Bakunin as there is for reggae; as much space for X as for poetic euphemisms in Ayuujk.

This mix of influences is one of the most refreshing and admirable characteristics of Yásnaya's intellectual work, and of the work of some of her Indigenous language-speaking intellectual companions – creatives, academics, and activists such as Luna Mará, Josefa Sánchez and Tajëëw Díaz. Their words, their creations, their acts are essentially at odds with the static, essentialist conceptions of original peoples, the mestizo obsession with seeing them only as heirs to and custodians of an ancient tradition rather than as living, changing cultures that are as modern – or even more so – than 'national' culture itself. For a decade, both she and her companions have been harnessing the power of social media and new information technologies to create one of the most vibrant and original areas of communication in our media landscape. This book is destined to be a model for the authentic flourishing and revival of contemporary thinking in Indigenous languages.

28 July, 2020

# THE ORIGINAL TEXTS, THE VOICE AND THE VOICES:

# INTRODUCTION TO BE READ AT THE END

Ana Aguilar Guevara, Julia Bravo Varela,
Gustavo Ogarrio Badillo and
Valentina Quaresma Rodríguez

*Ää plus **yuujk** becomes **ayuujk**, or plus **maxän** becomes **amaxän**. **Amaxän** would be 'the language of smallpox', i.e. Spanish; sorry, I mean, the language of all things sacred, though it does share a name with smallpox. And **Ayuujk** is the forest tongue, but if you add **ää** to it, the euphemism **ää ayuujk** means 'language', though **ää** also means 'mouth', so in a sense, for me, it's a way of saying 'this mouth is mine'.*

Who is Yásnaya? Granddaughter, reader, collector of books, notebooks, mugs, thread, plants and friends, workshop leader, educator, translator, defender, migrant, blogger, X user, Facebook user, sower of seeds, walker, community member, embroiderer, organiser of and commentator on festivities, teacher, maker of tamales,

9

tortillas and moles, activist, writer, linguist…

*Where was I born? I was born in San Pedro y San Pablo Ayutla, Mixe, in the Sierra Norte of Oaxaca, in the Mixe region. And this is where I grew up… I lived here until I was fifteen, without ever leaving. When I started high school I went to live in Texcoco, in the State of Mexico. Then from there I commuted to Mexico City while I was doing my undergraduate degree. At the end of my degree I moved to Mexico City.*

Any definition we might hazard of her political and writerly activity would be inexact and probably pointless because both the texts collected here and Yásnaya's later work are naturally at odds with notions defining intellectual and political fields. They are expressed in a time and a place whose process does not chime with or, importantly, make reference to, the ways our habitual genealogies of thought were defined.

Her individual voice is also the trace of a community voice. Its place of enunciation is, for that very reason, a political space, thanks to the tension between her *I* and that *we* in the Sierra Norte and in other towns and communities that share a similar topos, between the individual and the communal, between language and the autonomic process. Her trajectory runs from Ayutla to Mexico City, from Mixe to Spanish, but always within the political and cultural matrix that defines her: Ayuujk.

*I didn't go to kindergarten but I did go to Alma Campesina primary school. And, I guess, even when I lived in Mexico City I was always visiting Ayutla. I started certain projects during the periods I spent here, in Ayutla, where I live now… after finishing my degree and spending five or six years in Mexico City. After that I moved to Oaxaca City and lived there for four years, and I'd come to Ayutla at the weekends. And since 2015, the end of 2015, I came back to live in Ayutla, where I still am. I also went to secondary school here. I went to high school at the Escuela Preparatoria Texcoco; did my degree in Hispanic Language and Literatures and my master's in Hispanic Linguistics at the UNAM. My first language, my mother tongue, is Mixe. I started learning Spanish when I first went to school, when I was about six... or seven years old.*

Here we have the outline of an education, a working life, a way of thinking and a language that always have their *here*. And that *here*, which is Ayutla and the Ayuujk language, accompanies her texts, ideas and experiences, and her way of promoting linguistic diversity in a country like Mexico; in a context of structural violence against peoples and communities defending their territories.

*Well, when I was in Texcoco I worked at a stall that sold hats and, I remember well, watches, and I learned how to change the batteries and fix the straps. Later I got scholarships for a number of research projects. I worked at the National Institute of Indigenous Languages for nine months. I also worked in the National Institute of Adult Education developing grammar content in textbooks to teach adults in Indigenous languages. I participated in a project documenting endangered languages, with Elena Ibáñez; and in projects documenting Mixe. Then I went back to Oaxaca, to the capital, and worked there in the Juan de Córdova Research Library, a specialist research library and archive of Indigenous culture and languages; I was in charge of cultural development there. Since then, well, I've devoted myself instead to writing and giving workshops on a more freelance basis.*

In 2015, Yásnaya was invited to give a lecture titled *Indigenous Literature or Literature in Indigenous Languages?* to members of the Faculty of Philosophy and Letters at the UNAM. On this return trip to the university, she spoke about poetic expression in Indigenous languages that are invisible to a literary canon that conceives literature as universal. She also shared a way of thinking about linguistic diversity from the perspective of community activism, one that combined social media with the tools of a university education. The lecture was framed by a series of academic events discussing the 'pride' still provoked by Spanish having become one of the four languages most often spoken natively around the world, even though this statistic implies the loss of hundreds of languages as a consequence of a historical human rights violation. The event coincided with the one-year anniversary of the forced disappearance of students from the Escuela Normal Rural in Ayotzinapa, some of whom come from Nahua, Mixtec, Amuzgo, Huave and Zapotec communities. In a long and moving question and answer session, we saw Yásnaya engage with people the same way she engages every day on social media with web users of every stripe who have found her posts to give powerful insight into the problems arising among state figures, nations and languages. This book was conceived as a way of providing a 'permanent' place for those ephemeral texts (though what could be more permanent than their enduring echo in the minds of those who have interacted with them?).

> *But now it seems like it will really happen. I start in San Juan Guichicovi in the Isthmus of Tehuantepec (three hundred metres above sea level) and finish in my hometown, San Pedro y San Pablo Ayutla (two thousand three hundred metres above sea level). In*

*between I'll do what I've always imagined my grand-parents doing, though I suppose it will be different because I'm setting off on the journey when walking is no longer necessary – belatedly, I guess, because many of the paths either became roads or dirt tracks or just disappeared. But a lot of them do still exist. The end goal of climbing two thousand metres in two months is to see the sunset from Anaajëntump, the place of thunder, which, for those who don't know, is the highest*

*mountain in the photo in the header of this blog and the highest mountain in my people's region. And naturally we will have a party to celebrate the return of the relics from the sanctuary, and absolutely everyone is invited.*[1]

The entire initial section of this book, 'Written Language, Typed Language', brings together a series of essays, linguistic microfictions and social media posts that, at the risk of simplifying their discursive complexity, we have grouped together as *manifestos*. This heterogeneity of written expression is characteristic of Yásnaya's reflections during her first years of publishing in *Este País* (between 2011 and 2015) as well as on Facebook and X (formerly Twitter). Both the issues she tackles in them as well as her style of argument and narration break with the 'standard-ising' formats used to convey political thinking or write up academic research: the anecdotal evolves into critical reflection, the everyday becomes part of her thinking, and an event that seems simple, circumstantial, or ordinary

---

[1] Thus began Yásnaya's journey through the Mixe region in the summer of 2009 and the blog that she kept along the way. The opening entry, to which this quotation belongs, can be consulted at: Mutsk Len (17 June, 2009). 'El amanecer desde Anaajëntump' [Blog post]. XËNË'M NOJTY JA' ET. La ruta ayuujk.

can spark innumerable meanings which are, once again, political. What's more, her episodic style problematises the labels imposed by the (western) literary canon onto what could be, but definitively is not, a discursive and/or literary genre. Potential concepts are subtly insinuated into the narrative and the conversation, perhaps in the hope that what the author has experienced and analysed might be reimagined or changed in some way.

To these manifestos two further sections are added. One of them comprises the speech titled 'Nëwemp, ja nëëj jëts ja ää Ayuujk' ('Mexico: The Water and the Word'), which Yásnaya delivered in the Mexican Congress's Chamber of Deputies to mark 2019 as the United Nations International Year of Indigenous Languages; this text, as  well as reflecting on the health of languages in Mexico, denounces the violent deprivation of potable water Ayutla has been experiencing since 2017.[2] Lastly, the book closes with an Epilogue, in which Yásnaya offers a retrospective opinion of her own writing.

*I do things relating to my presence here, to community life, when the Assembly entrusts me with specific things… there's that, and developing the community education projects I've been tasked with. I'm also on social media. I write for different media, usually for* Este País, *but also now for* El País *and for* Gatopardo. *And sometimes I'm asked to give a workshop. I belong to a collective called COLMIX, of young Mixes who work on different topics relating to the region, and they have community projects too. I love talking – I think*

---

[2]    For the details, as described by Yásnaya herself, see: Aguilar, Y. (June 2020). 'Agua con A de Ayutla: Una denuncia'. *Revista de la Universidad de México.*

*it's one of the things I most like doing – I like walking, going to the forest, I like planting, I love reading, embroidery. Going to community festivities or helping to organise community events… like, if we're going to put on such-and-such an event then I'll get involved alongside the other organisers, in self-generated projects coordinated by others, or wherever there's room for me to get involved. I love going to festivities and doing my bit in community initiatives. I love that, there are always parties.*

The texts span topics from the contradictions of living in one of the world's most linguistically diverse countries where most of its institutions and inhabitants conduct themselves as though it were not, to the problem of state violence against languages and the processes of autonomy currently allowing peoples and communities to resist. Ideas 'are talked through' and conceptualised as weapons against hegemonic concepts within linguistics, culture, politics and daily life itself. They engage in hand-to-hand combat with commonplaces that form part of the symbolic violence against speakers of languages other than Spanish.

In this way, sometimes emphatically and sometimes indirectly, Yásnaya tackles situations and problems relating to biculturalism and linguistic diversity. At the same time, she questions that ideological macro-category presented as the key to making peoples, communities and nations uniform: the 'Indigenous'. Similarly, she makes claims that articulate her understanding of languages in political terms. For example: 'a language without a state behind it is automatically at risk of disappearing.'

*What projects do I have on the go? Ooof… there are loads. There are community projects, all to do with*

*establishing a centre for the UNAM here in the town,
which is, like, a big project. But there's one I'm really
interested in, which is to set up a primary school. I hope
I can make it work. And there are some books I want
to write in Mixe, and some in Spanish, I want to do
that too.*

'As is the case with Mexico and France, the nation
states into which the world finds itself divided were
built on the assumption of homogeneity. A single nation
presupposes the existence of a single language,' Yásnaya
asserts. You'll find here plenty of heresy against the criollo
legacy that continues to underpin the Mexican state, as
well as a radical way of naming and tackling certain 'myths'
that sustain hegemonic monolingualism and are bound
up with the public policies responsible for dismantling
linguistic diversity in Mexico. There is a critical equation
underlying Yásnaya's reflections: the de facto language
of Mexico – 'Castilian' or Spanish – has the backing of
the nation state, and this implies the periodic exercise of
violence against other languages and nations.

*Where do I want to live when I'm old…? Well,
the primary school I was telling you about will be
monolingual, with Spanish or another language taught
as a second language. It'll be a very Mixe project with
a very Mixe vision, I want it to be really high quality,
I want it to be ours, to create our own education system.
And I'm interested in any project to do with self-gov-
ernance and community autonomy.*

This book is no dutiful tour of Yásnaya's writing.
Mainly it seeks answers from readers to certain urgent
questions. For example: how do we define linguistic
diversity in Mexico, and what is the state of that diversity?

What relationship do Mexico's inhabitants have with linguistic diversity? Why and how do languages become extinct? What implications do these losses have for the lives of their speakers? What actions, attitudes and political structures are responsible for them? What actions, attitudes and political structures can prevent them? Every piece in this collection tries to provoke a response in the reader, even the author's biographical details spilled onto these introductory pages. As well as contextualising her thinking, Yásnaya's own story illustrates opportunities for resistance, for preventing a common but certainly not unavoidable tragedy: that of a grandmother monolingual in an Indigenous language, a mother bilingual in an Indigenous language and Spanish, and a granddaughter monolingual in Spanish.

*OK, so now finally, where do I want to live when I'm old? That's easy: ever since I returned to Ayutla I've wanted to live here, here is where I want to be, I want to die here, I want to be buried with my grandmother, where my grandmother is. What do I want to do when I'm old? I want to have time to read and to do my planting. What I'd most like to do as an old woman is plant things. I don't want much, I don't think. I want to be here. If my Gran were here things would be better. I want to live here. It's a bit strange talking about myself.*

30 July, 2020

(Yásnaya Aguilar)

# Has no idea where to begin…

# Bursting in on someone, out of the blue…

# WRITTEN LANGUAGE,
# TYPED LANGUAGE

## PART I:
## PRIDE AND PREJUDICES

# TO BE OR NOT TO BE?: BILINGUALISMS

There were, I remember, two kinds of primary school in my hometown and the rest of the region: the 'formal education' schools, where all subjects were taught in Spanish, and 'bilingual schools', where lessons were taught in Ayuujk (until we had mastered Spanish). The official attitude towards this second type of school was – how shall I put it? – peculiar. Parents generally believed they should avoid sending their children to bilingual schools because it was said they'd receive a lower quality of education there. These schools had more precarious facilities and the bilingual teachers received a much lower salary than teachers in the 'formal' system, where they taught lessons in just one language: Spanish. This was despite most of us children speaking Ayuujk as our mother tongue. Needless to say, the bilingual teachers tried to move into the 'formal' system whenever they could. The word *bilingual* was understood to have negative connotations – to be the opposite of 'formal'.

On my first trip to Mexico City – I had by then learned to read Spanish – I realised, inferring from various adverts and certain conversations, that there were bilingual schools there, too, but that people actively tried to send their children there and that their teachers earned higher salaries. Bilingual secretaries were valued more highly than monolingual ones and I realised that, generally speaking, that same word *bilingual* had positive connotations. And as I've said before, for a moment I thought, as did my little sister back then, that in addition to Spanish most people living in Mexico City also spoke Nahuatl and that it was held in very high regard.

> Most of Mexico's population is monolingual in Spanish; most Indigenous people are bilingual.
>
> 𝕏        *11 Aug, 2014*

Soon it was explained to me that no, *bilingual* meant being able to speak two languages: in this case, English and Spanish. It was then I realised that the issue wasn't the fact of speaking two languages, but *which* two languages you spoke. I realised there were different classes of bilingualism and that at least one of them seemed to be undesirable: if you were a teacher, speaking an Indigenous language implied having a lower salary and less prestige within the education system.

To put it simply, I came to understand that being bilingual is not the same as being *bilingual*.

4 Jan, 2012

# THE CENSORING OF BABEL

Turns out it's difficult, if not impossible, to appreciate something you have no idea exists. Someone told me a story that, as I see it, proves that one of the cruellest aspects of discrimination against speakers of different languages is the denial of their existence. When a friend of mine accompanied his grandfather to a different town, he noticed that, when interacting with friends, his grandfather used words he didn't understand. When asked about it outright, his grandfather explained that he spoke 'Mexican' with his friends. That was how, having lived in close quarters with him for several years, my friend finally learned that his grandfather was one of their community's last surviving Nahuatl speakers.

As things stand, it's clear that in monolingual contexts you're much more likely to learn of the existence of Japanese or Russian, to name two geographically distant

*My grandmother NEVER ceases to surprise me. Example no. 19.*
*Me: You have a new puppy!!! He's so cute!!! What's his name???*
*Gran: Näp top.*
*Me: Näp top??? What does that mean???*
*Gran: Laptop in Mixe. I called him that because I hope he'll be as quick and intelligent as those machines you lot are always using. Ba-dum-tss.*

 *11 Dec, 2012*

*Conversations with my Gran:*
*G: What's with that giant book?!!*
*It's fatter than the Bible.*
*Y: Errr, it's an encyclopaedic dictionary of English.*
*G: And have you started reading it?*
*Y: You don't really read it, you just look stuff up…*
*G: That's not true, your grand-father read the entire dictionary. Don't you remember he used to make you read it, too? And people would be furious because he'd send them letters using words from the dictionary that no one understood. So don't lie, just say you can't be bothered.*
*Y: Well, yes, you're right, but…*
*G: But nothing, get reading, because if you don't you might never finish it. You're not exactly young any more…*
*Thanks for the dictionary, Krissel Maclay!*

🅕                              *7 Sept, 2016*

languages, than to learn that there is a language called Matlatzinca spoken in the State of Mexico. By doing a brief, informal survey of the first time my friends realised languages other than their mother tongue (in most cases, Spanish) were spoken elsewhere in the world, I realised English was the first 'other language' they became aware of. Whether it was school, songs by the Beatles, TV programmes, or a grandfather who did seasonal work in the US, the first time they realised that not all the world's humans speak the same language was because of English.

When it comes to bilingual or multilingual families, the story is different. I know a girl who lives in a Spanish-speaking city, asks her mother for things in Italian, tells her dad stories in English and then explains her drawings to me in Spanish. For her, you could say, it's the existence of a pre-Babelian world that would be strange. In my case, as well as knowing of the existence of Spanish, I knew about Zapotec and Chinantec from people who came to the local market. I

26

wonder about kids who grow up in Tlapa, a city in the state of Guerrero where Nahuatl, Spanish, Mixtec and Me'phaa (also known as Tlapanec) are spoken every day, how aware of language diversity they are.

I've come to realise that, even though Mexico's big cities are home to many speakers of its different languages, it's the urban spaces with Spanish-speaking populations that contain the least information about the country's linguistic diversity. I think this situation is closely connected to a systematic, though invisible, censorship of Mexico's languages. As far as the school system goes, it's more important to know – and often to have learned off by heart – the country's state capitals than the names of Mexico's languages and the places where they're spoken. Why is cultural and linguistic diversity not a key topic in learning materials? Seeing as it isn't, I still often meet people who are surprised to know Maya didn't stop being spoken in the pre-Hispanic era or that other languages aren't just dialects. That most people don't at least know the names of the languages spoken in their country or their state is staggering, to say the least, as is the surprise people show when they discover, for example, that the last five speakers of the Kiliwa language live in Baja California, and that they, too, are Mexicans. The country's diverse Indigenous cultures were for years subsumed under the label 'campesino' in reference to often impoverished rural workers – similarly, its language diversity has been hidden within the category of 'dialect'.

If we don't even know linguistic diversity exists, it's hard for us to ask for more information, to demand spaces where we can learn about and enjoy the languages spoken in our own country. Overcoming the censorship of different languages is a necessary, crucial first step towards building a multilingual society. This censorship affects us all – both those who speak censored languages and those who, despite living in this country, have never heard of the existence of, say, Guarijio.

So what about you: how did you learn that languages other than Spanish are spoken in this country?

29 Nov, 2012

# THE RINGING OF BELLS:
# TWO ENCOUNTERS WITH
# THE LANGUAGE OF
# THE OTHER

I.

In Ayutla Mixe, 'tääy' means 'to be amusing/to be funny/ to be witty', while in Tlahuitoltepec Mixe it means 'to lie'. A subtle difference that in certain contexts has got me into a fix: 'are you lying to me?' someone will ask, and I understand 'are you being funny?', to which I reply, enthusiastically and with a wink, 'yes'. Somewhere

> In Mixe, blue and green are just shades of the same colour: tsujxk. That's why I can only tell you what my favourite colour is in my mother tongue.
>
> 𝕏                    28 May, 2016

between lying and being witty lies fiction – the common denominator from which each 'communalect', to use a term coined by Leopoldo Valiñas, particularised the word's meaning.[3] Similarly, in Ayutla Mixe, 'anu'kx' is the verb 'to be tired', while in Tlahuitoltepec Mixe it means

---

3    Leopoldo Valiñas Coalla is a linguist and researcher at the Institute for Anthropological Research at the UNAM. He coined the term *communalect* to describe the linguistic system used by a particular community of speakers.

'to sweat', and this slight but obvious difference has also led to some amusing anecdotes. Plus, what for me means 'kind' – 'tuta'aky' – for them means 'slow'. An encounter with the Other (as many books whose titles now escape me have said) can lead to profound self-knowledge, and this is true of my dealings with other Ayuujk 'communalects'. Without the – intense, of late – periods of time spent with friends from Xaamkëjxp (Tlahuitoltepec), I would never have stopped to think about the stream of Mixe words that spills from my mouth, would not have been surprised at the fine differences, wouldn't have reached hypotheses about the origins of words. In short, I wouldn't have learned about myself, about how I speak, through the lens, the eyes and the language of others.

## II.

My grandmother is eighty, and we're always having the most stimulating conversations about our mother tongue:

*In Mixe, as in English, 'querer' and 'amar' are expressed using a single word meaning 'to love'. 'Kajaanaxy mejts ntseky' is both to suffer and to enjoy, ;).*

X                    24 Mar, 2016

Gran: A friend told me her son doesn't want to go to school any more. He says that now there are kids who speak Mixe from other communities and it annoys him. It annoys him that everyone else speaks differently, that they don't speak normally.

Y: Did you say anything to him?

Gran: Yes, I explained to the boy that just as Mixe from other communities seems strange, funny or unpleasant to us, they probably think the same about the Mixe we speak. There is no normal Mixe, they are all different and all lovely. Do you know why?

Y: No. I mean, yes. I mean, no.

Gran: It's because of the church bells. Every town has its own bell tower, and they all ring with their own unique sound; the people who live there hear them tolling every day and the sound stays in their minds, affecting the shape of their words, giving them their character. That's why every community's Mixe is different – unique, just like their bell tower.

23 June, 2014

# HABITS OF SPEECH

*When identity is called into doubt,*
*action becomes paralysed*

Sheba Camacho

I still don't understand the relationship between a person's mother tongue and their identity. It always seems so complex, so I go off on a tangent or get up on my soapbox, unable to come to any conclusion; and things are even more

*Tukyo'm, my town, nestled on the mountain, shaded with trees and leaves, like a piggy bank where we kept our memories. You'll see why a person would want to live there for an eternity. The dawn, the morning, the afternoon, and the night were always the same; except for changes in the air. The air changes the colour of things there; where life whirs by as if it were a murmur; as if it were a pure murmur of life.[4]*

🅕                      *13 Nov, 2016*

[4] This entry is a modified excerpt from *Pedro Páramo*, the novel by Juan Rulfo, which reads: 'My town, nestled on the plain, shaded with trees and leaves, like a piggy bank where we kept our memories. You'll see why a person would want to live there for an eternity. The dawn, the morning, the afternoon, and the night, were always the same; except for changes in the air. The air changes the colour of things there; where life whirs by as if it were a murmur; as if it were a pure murmur of life…' J. Rulfo, *Pedro Páramo*, translated by Armand F. Baker (2015).

complex when the question is directed, threateningly, towards what was, or still is, my own process. In Europe I was Mexican, in Mexico I'm Oaxacan, in Oaxaca I'm Mixe, in the highlands I'm from Ayutla. At some point or other I'm Indigenous but that's something I was told or that I intuited through comparison before the label was attached to me. In an alien invasion I would undoubtedly be an Earth-dweller, and an enthusiastic one at that. I cannot understand identity without contrasts, because with every new contrast a new identity is born in me: 'turns out I'm Latina, too, now, eh?' Since humans are fortunate enough to be able to speak more than one language (the possibility of not being able to makes me panic), the relationship between language and identity can never be deterministic; somewhere, the two things overlap to form a subset, but an unstable one that swells or slips away depending on the person.

Officially speaking, to describe yourself as Indigenous is enough to be considered as such. However, in reality, and for statistical purposes, the only people who count as Indigenous are those who speak a language belonging to one of the eleven linguistic families that were spoken in what is now Mexican territory before Cortés arrived with Indo-European on his lips. When asked outright, my grandmother denies being Indigenous – she is Ayuujk, she says, no question about it, the people of the mountain tongue. For me, the world was divided in two, and the division was obvious: if you didn't speak Ayuujk, you had to be 'akäts' (not Mixe); whether you were Japanese, Swiss, Tarahumara, Guarani or Zapotec, all were known as 'akäts'. It's no coincidence that in most Indigenous languages there's no word for 'Indigenous'. By establishing many new, simultaneous contrasts, I realised that behind that word there's a whole hidden network, a network that can be deceptive.

'My mother says I'm not Mixe any more', I heard someone say, to my surprise, some weeks ago, '...because I don't speak in Ayuujk any more, I can't call myself that.' I asked a couple of questions and then, after many mezcals, we concluded that she's as Ayuujk as the mist hanging over Zempoaltépetl (sacred mountain); that she is a Spanish-speaking Mixe. That's right, M-i-x-e, as we are known in Spanish. Who's to say otherwise?

Movements that seek recognition for Indigenous communities tend to use the revitalisation of their languages as a battle cry. But one extreme consequence of this can be contempt – sometimes tacit, sometimes overt – for those who have lost their language. It's not that they don't have a mother tongue – their mother tongue is Spanish. As I see it, it is essential that the processes of linguistic revitalisation and strengthening avoid resorting to the same mechanisms that were used to impose Spanish; if we want there to be a basic consistency to our claims and in our fight for an intercultural society, we can't rule somebody out for speaking Spanish.

Despite this tendency towards linguistic lynching, I've found that the children of many Indigenous leaders don't speak their original language, or can only under-stand it. Their parents know full well its importance; how losing that language means cutting off a direct route of knowledge transmission. They know that in the current context, to speak an Indigenous language is to imply resistance. There's no lack of ideology, so what's going on? I'm not remotely interested in judging this phenomenon, but I'd like to be able to explain it. It's not enough, it would seem, to take an ideological stance on a language. Being proud of your mother tongue, appreciating it, understanding it, can't guarantee you'll be able to pass it on to your children. Once again, I ask: what's going on? Only this time, even more intrigued. Eventually I arrive at the following: speaking a language is also a habit, an automatic, everyday practice, and once initial interactions have been established in one language they turn out, as with any habit, to be difficult to change. I have a friend with whom, for some reason, I always speak in Ayuujk, despite knowing he speaks perfect Spanish; and another friend, who I got to know more recently in the city, with whom for some reason I always speak in Spanish, even though I know perfectly well that Ayuujk is her mother tongue and she speaks it every day, just not with me. These aren't conscious decisions, we don't choose to make them, or at least not entirely.

What about people who learn three languages simultaneously as children? What role does each of their languages play in the construction of their identity? What's the relationship between language and identity in native speakers of English? I don't know. I said earlier that our mother tongue is woven into the fabric of our identity but does not determine it until a contrast is established; I said all that, but the truth is I can't help being happy when, after hearing me speak, someone from another town in the Mixe highlands says to me: 'OK, you look akäts but you speak Ayuujk so you must be one of us… go on then, which community are you from?' Whenever this happens, I invariably smile in relief.

11 April, 2012

# INDIGENOUS LANGUAGES WRITE THEIR LETTER TO THE THREE WISE MEN

Dear Wise Men,

We've been very good this year. Hang on, what are we saying?! We've been good for over five hundred years, against all odds. So good that you'll understand if our list looks a bit demanding. We trust in your generosity.

1. We'd like, next year, for all Mexicans to know what to call us, where we live, and what we sound like.

   *Mexico is weird: most of its inhabitants can't name the languages spoken in their own country.*

   𝕏         *26 Aug, 2014*

2. Please bring us patience so we can get along nicely with Spanish. We like her, but we suspect someone's making her push us around. We'll share our toys and play with her, we don't mind.
3. We want to be allowed to go to school. We want to take our rucksack full of curious sounds. We don't like that kids have to hide us in the classroom. A lot of them are still punished when they hang out with us on school property.

*If anthologies and edited volumes of 'Mexican' literature are anything to go by, after Nezahualcoyotl nobody wrote literature in Indigenous languages ever again.*

X                    *11 Sept, 2014*

4. Books! We love books. We used to get given loads, but now we've got hardly any. Actually, it would be even better if you could bring each of us a bunch of printing presses. That way books can be published in all possible Mexican languages.

5. A computer with an internet connection for each of us – that way we can start blogs, edit Wikipedia pages, have our own websites. The internet could be filled with our characters!

6. We want the gift of ubiquity. We'd like to be everywhere: in hospitals, in courts, in town squares, on TV and the radio, but mainly, always, in the mouths of children and anyone who might want to speak us.

Basically, we'd like all the same toys languages like German, English and Japanese have. We're all languages, we all have the same rights.

We know you're coming from really far away and that our presents might take a while to get here, but don't give up. We'll leave some water out for the camel, peanuts for the elephant and hay for the horse.

With love,
The Indigenous languages of Mexico

19 Dec, 2013

# AYUUJK: SO LINGUISTIC DIVERSITY HAS A GREAT FUTURE AHEAD OF IT? TIME, SPACE AND METAPHORS

It's almost impossible to talk about time without using spatial metaphors: the future that lies ahead, the past we left behind. In front, behind, timelines that move on horizontal planes. The linguist Martina Faller says that in the Quechua language, and in Aymara, temporal metaphors are different: the past, which we already know, is in front of us, before our eyes, while the future, uncertain, is behind our backs, where we can't see it. The language we use shapes the way we talk about time, the way we detail it. In the case of Mixe, time

*One of the nicest things about living in Tukyo'm is that the phrase 'I've brought you a little something' might mean someone's giving you: some long strips of venison, or...*

*a portion of freshly baked agave leaves, or...*

*a large serving of hot, fresh, sweet pumpkin, or...*

*a pot of flowering, almost-ripe strawberries, or...*

*a tea towel full of tortillas straight off the comal, or...*

*a large bag of freshly baked bread, or...*

*a basket of fragrant lemons, or...*

*a bag of freshly steamed chayotes, or...*

*a bag of coffee, freshly roasted on the comal, or...*

*a bottle of mezcal de olla, or...*

*The possibilities are endless. Timy tyoskujuyëp.*

❶         7 Feb, 2016

is also understood spatially, except that this space isn't horizontal, it's vertical; time runs through us from our head to our feet, it falls on top of us: we say 'ka't yaknajäw tii menp këtäkp' ('we don't know what's coming down') or 'menp pajtp' ('it's coming, it's rising'). Changing from Mixe to Spanish involves moving from a vertical to a horizontal plane when speaking metaphorically.

In Spanish we use nouns such as 'el porvenir' (literally, 'that which is to come') for the future and say 'vamos a bailar' (literally, 'we are going to dance' to mean 'let's dance') or 'vamos a pensar' or 'vamos a descansar', using a verb of motion, 'ir' ('to go'), a verb that moves through space in order to refer to time. Time, as we now know well, is relative. It is established at the moment of speech. If I'm speaking on 18 August, 1934, then 18 August, 1981 will be in the future; if I'm speaking on 18 August, 1989, that same day will be in the past. In both cases, it's the same date: 18 August, 1981. It was in the future the day my grandmother was born, and the past the year my grandfather died.

Time is codified in language in many ways, from how we talk about it to the words we associate with its passing and even the patterns of conjugation in verb endings, such as those in Spanish: como, comí, comeré, I eat, I ate, I will eat. These verbs change if we move from the past to the present or the future – their form is sensitive to that change. In contrast, verbs in Mixe change their endings depending on the temporal structure of the actions to which we're referring: finished events are all marked in the same way, whether they take place in the past or in the future:

| Tëë näjty **y'etsy** | (she will have danced) | FUTURE |
| Tëë **y'etsy** | (she has already danced) | PAST |

Unlike in Spanish, where the verb ending changes depending on whether we're referring to the past or future, verbs in Mixe (marked above in bold) do not. In both examples the verb is the same; it doesn't change, because in both examples we're talking about actions that have finished. As you'll see in the following examples, the form of the verb 'to dance' (in bold) changes when we're talking about uncompleted actions and looks the same regardless of whether they're in the past or the future.

| **Ajtsp** näjty japom | (tomorrow she will be dancing) | FUTURE |
| **Ajtsp** näjty axëëy | (yesterday she was dancing) | PAST |

The form the Mixe verbs take is indifferent to the past or future, but it cares about time in a different way – it cares whether or not actions are complete:

| Tëë **y'etsy** | (she danced yesterday) | PAST, COMPLETE |
| **Ajtsp** näjty axëëy | (she was dancing yesterday) | PAST, INCOMPLETE |

Even when both verbs happened in the past, Mixe continues to mark them differently. The verb changes according to the sound that's played; in Spanish, the sound of past–present–future is crucial, while Mixe verbs dance to the sound of the internal temporal structure of the action, whether it has been completed or not. This particular way of marking time is known as aspect. Languages such as Mixe, Maya and Russian are languages of aspect, with verbs that are indifferent to the contrasts between past, present and future.

How do we know, then, in Mixe, whether an action is happening in the past or in the future, if the verb remains so nonchalantly in the same form? We know because of the context, or because it's indicated using other words rather than reflected in the verb form itself. Time is always there, it's just marked differently in each language. Moving from a language such as Mixe to a language such as Spanish implies making a change in the temporal system that's marked as verb variation.

To return to where we began, linguists say the use of space to talk about time is a universal trait. But since I've always been a rebel, I've been refusing, trying instead to think and speak about time in another way, whether in Mixe or in Spanish. But it turns out it's hard; turns out I can't. Have you ever tried?

24 July, 2015

# DO I SPEAK MIXE OR AYUUJK? ON THE NAMING AND SELF-DESIGNATION OF INDIGENOUS LANGUAGES AND PEOPLES

'Mixe' is a Mixe word. 'Mixe', the word currently used to designate my people and the language I speak, was taken from Mixe languages by Zapotec speakers to describe us. 'Mixe' comes from the Mixe word 'mijxy', 'child' or 'boy'. Through historical chance, this word, now Hispanicised, ending up being the one used to name us: Mixe. A word from Mixe that meant 'child' was taken by Zapotecs to denote a neighbouring community, their first great 'other', and from there it travelled into Spanish to designate that same community as well as the language varieties they speak. The word 'mijxy' still has its original meaning today: 'child' or 'boy', and most speakers don't know that it shares its etymology with the Spanish word 'mixe'.

Many years ago, I referred to a friend as 'tlapaneco'. Offended, he explained to me that he wasn't Tlapanec, he was Me'phaa. He talked of a pejorative etymology attributed to the name given to his people in Spanish and the importance of using their self-designation. What's more, he said, 'you're not Mixe, you're ayuujk jä'äy'. This statement made me consider the complex web in which Indigenous peoples and languages are inscribed and to which we must attend in the act of naming and referring to them. My first reaction was to reply that I respected the fact my friend didn't want to be called Tlapanec but at the same time I wasn't offended if someone referred to me as Mixe. In the word Tlapanec my friend read something very different to me. He read the word's etymological meaning, its origin and the pejorative charge attributed to it. In that same word, I read a designation; for me the meaning of the word Tlapanec was the people themselves, their language: I characterised my friend as belonging to the former and as a speaker of the latter. I could not 'activate', so to speak, the word's pejorative charge because I didn't know its context, origin or etymology. Similarly, neither could I feel offended by being called Mixe, because I found no pejorative charge in the etymology of the word, which is often used by people in my community to describe ourselves when speaking in our own language.

Indigenous peoples, not 'Indigenous groups.' The legal implications are very different.

X                18 April, 2012

Since this incident many years ago, I've noticed increased recognition of Indigenous peoples' and languages' self-designations. That said, as ever, the issue is complex, and the use of self-designations comes with its own difficulties. On the one hand we have to consider that, unlike with names in Spanish, Indigenous languages usually make a clear distinction between the name for the language and the name for the people. In Spanish, a person is 'huave' and speaks 'huave', but according to the self-denomination that same person is 'ikoots' but speaks 'ombeayüts' – just as a Uruguayan does not speak Uruguayan, but rather

Spanish. In Mixe, I am 'ayuujk jä'äy' and I speak 'ayuujk', in Seri people are 'comcáac' and they speak 'cmiique iitom'.

However, when using Indigenous people's self-designations in Spanish we must take certain things into account. If we want Indigenous languages to be treated the same as all other languages in the world, then we'd have to use the self-designations of all those languages too. We'd have to banish the term 'inglés' from Spanish and only use 'English', say 'français' instead of 'francés', and the same for all the rest. Failure to be consistent in the way we name languages (using self-designations for Indigenous languages but not for the languages of other nation states) could continue to reinforce the political and social differences that underpin the category of 'Indigenous language'. Do we really want that?

On the other hand, we cannot ignore that the origins of many of these names are charged with prejudice; 'popoluca', for example, is a name in Nahuatl that alludes to an incomprehensible language, something garbled. However, I'm sure that when the speakers of Popoluca use that word they are referring to the language and not activating its possible pejorative charge. After all, offence resides in intention more than in words; for an offence to take place, the intention to offend and the taking of offence are both necessary. No wonder you can offend someone deeply by using the word 'querida' – 'dear' or 'love' – in the right context and with the right intonation.

The names used in Spanish for Indigenous languages come from other languages and via different processes, some with pejorative origins, others without them; many come from Nahuatl, but others do not. At first, these names were assigned to peoples rather than to languages (see my article titled 'On the Names of

45

Languages', parts I and II).[5]

Another risk when using self-designations is that we legitimate certain language varieties over others: it's not the same to be a speaker of 'ayuujk', 'ayuuk', 'ayöök', 'ëyuuk' or 'ayuk'. In my experience, the choice of name is related to the visibility of certain variants or communities over others for reasons that are extralinguistic. When we choose among these names, which variants and differences are we invisibilising? When we choose among these names, which communities and language varieties feel they are not represented? Unlike when we say Mixe, choosing the self-designation 'ayuujk' over 'ayuuk' implies referring only to varieties of Mixe spoken in certain communities in the southern Mixe highlands.

When speaking in Spanish, I speak 'mixe'. When speaking in Mixe, I speak 'ayuujk', but not 'ayuuk'. You can call my language 'mixe' or 'ayuujk' when speaking in Spanish, either is fine with me. I understand the pejorative charge in other cases, and it must not be ignored, though that charge and etymology aren't always activated. When referring to other languages I choose the word preferred by my interlocutor – at the end of the day, that's what all this is about. ¿Cómo te llamas? What's your name, or rather, literally, what do you call yourself? *You* – what is *your* self-designation?

> *In Mixe, Mexico City is called Nëwemp, whose etymology is 'in the place of water'.*
>
> X        8 Nov, 2016

5 June, 2015

---

[5] The articles are available on the *Este País* website. https://estepais.com/.

# PRIDE AND PREJUDICES

At university I met Naomi Tokumasu, who had a Japanese mother, a Mexican father, and was inhabited by both Spanish and Japanese. It's strange – among the first things I asked her was if she could teach me a few phrases in Japanese, which she refused point blank to do, just as I would have liked to refuse every time someone asked me to teach them phrases in Mixe as soon as they met me. Despite being very different, over the years Naomi and I have built a friendship in which, as I see it, questions about identity and belonging have been a constant – questions that are reflected all over the place, that reverberate through the kaleidoscope of our affection for each other. Naomi and I have in common the basic fact of being different; of standing out.

*We all have our own Ithaca and mine is called Tukyo'm (Ayutla).*

X                    *28 Mar, 2014*

It's no surprise, then, that of all my friends it's been with her that topics such as belonging, culture shock and identity have begun to take on new dimensions. While drinking tea at her place one time, I asked if she felt proud of being Japanese. She answered that she was glad she spoke Japanese. That simple response, uttered among the biscuits and between sips of tea, opened a floodgate of reflection in me.

It's common to hear in campaigns and in the mouths of the well-intentioned that we should be proud to speak Indigenous languages. 'Speak it with Pride', says one of the National Institute of Indigenous Languages's most recent campaigns. Pride can strengthen ties in a dignified way, but it can also be arrogant about it. In the worst of cases, it can be used as an emotional plaster over a deep, gaping wound. A way of padding out something that's missing.

> *Falling in love releases endorphins, does it? Try explaining Ayuujk grammar in Ayuujk... pure happiness.*
>
> ⓕ                    *27 July, 2016*

I understand that languages such as Mixe, Nahuatl and Mazahua have long been condemned to silence in many spaces. I know of one family that, whenever they got on the metro in Mexico City, would lower their voices so the Nahuatl they spoke loudly at home became a barely audible murmur. They never agreed to do this; it was something they did automatically. Faced with this situation, encouraging people to speak with pride seems a possible though very vague response.

> *¿Ka't meets m'amaxan xxëëtunä'- änt? Aren't you guys going to celebrate your Spanish? #dilm14 #Ayuujk #Mixe*
>
> 𝕏                    *21 Feb, 2014*

What does it mean to speak a language with pride? The connotations will be different from one language to another; proudly speaking English can obviously be read completely differently to proudly speaking Maya. Does it mean, maybe, that we won't lower our voices when we get on the metro, that we'll stop feeling ashamed to say words in a language that's subject to discrimination? No, it's something different. To be proudly Indigenous or to speak Mixe proudly is evidence of its lack of recognition, evidence of ongoing discrimination, evidence that what should be normal is not and needs to be reasserted. Claiming pride in being Indigenous confirms and embeds our subordinate position.

Thinking about all of this and citing Naomi, I want to be glad that I speak Mixe, to take pleasure in its labyrinthine morphology, to use it to express the most prosaic as well as the most sublime things. Pride is not the answer; the  answer is taking everyday enjoyment in it, so common-place that it's imperceptible, so imperceptible that there's no place for pride. Mixe, my mother tongue, is no better than any other language – it's no better than Spanish, it's no better than French. To have acquired it isn't a merit, it just happened because I was immersed in a world narrated in that language. I love it, I take pleasure in, the same way anyone  else loves their mother tongue, anyone who was never forced, on account of discrimination, to lower their voice when they got on the metro.

We have to change this subor-dinate relationship so that the metro or anywhere else can become a space where it is possible to speak a language with neither shame nor pride. Where it's as normal as breathing – breathing easy.

P.S. You can read some of Naomi Tokumasu's reflec-tions from Japan on the blog 'Gin Sin Tonic'.

24 April, 2014

# INDIGENOUS LITERATURE
# DOES NOT EXIST

I don't want to re-hash here the debate about the relevance of using the word *literature* to designate poetic production in Indigenous languages. It's a lot like the varied and conflicting arguments over whether the Aztec sun stone or the Coatlicue statue can or cannot be called art. I don't think there's much sense in arguing about whether a label corresponds or not to a particular phenomenon; rather, I'm interested in establishing the similarities and differences between poetic phenomena found in different languages, languages that are distant both geographically and in their genealogies.

> *Apparently everything sounds more poetic in Indigenous languages. Watch out now – that's just discrimination by way of idealisation.*
>
> X                    8 May, 2013

However, we can't ignore the fact that this category – *Indigenous literature* – is being used, and that this has several implications. You'll find a fair number of articles and essays referring to the current flourishing of Indigenous literature in Mexico; there's also the creation of the Nezahualcóyotl Prize for Literature in Indigenous Languages; and in 2012 the Guadalajara International Book Fair, one of the most important international book fairs, announced the creation of the Ibero-American Indigenous Literature Prize, worth 25,000 dollars.

These examples suggest Mexican literature is currently divided into literature produced in Spanish and literature produced in Indigenous languages. This division strikes me as illusory. Why would we assume that literature produced in Spanish is different to all other literatures produced in the great diversity of languages known as Indigenous? What literary trait distinguishes them? What literary trait shared by the poetics of Tarahumara and Zoque justifies consigning them to the same category? Why would we need to give a single literary prize to works in such different languages?[6] I don't believe there's any evidence for the existence of an Indigenous literature.

The only two traits Indigenous languages have in common are the following: they are descended from earlier languages that were spoken in a territory known today as Mexico, and they have long suffered discrimination. To assume that such different languages, belonging to eleven radically different phylogenetic groups, have the same poetic strategies which together can be contrasted with the poetic strategies

> *The fact that some hundred and fifty years ago most of the Spanish-speaking Mexican population was illiterate wasn't a valid reason to stop producing books in Spanish, was it? So why use that argument when it comes to Mexican languages?*
>
> ❶      28 Nov, 2012

---

[6] Yásnaya probably considers these languages to be so different because they belong to different linguistic families. Tarahumara is from the Uto-Aztecan family and Zoque is from the Mixe-Zoque family. The linguistic distance between these two languages is comparable, for example, to the distance between an Indo-European language such as Spanish, Kurdish or Farsi and a Mongolic language such as Kalmyk, or a Niger-Congo language such as Ibo.

of Spanish seems, based on the lack of evidence, unsustainable to me. The grammatical, linguistic and poetic strategies associated with each language, Indigenous or otherwise, are very different. The poetics of Mixe are as different to those of Spanish as they are to those of Seri. What's the real reason for grouping together the different literary manifestations of these languages? Perhaps people believe Indigenous languages are unable to compete for the same prizes. Perhaps people believe their literary traditions are too young, that they lack poetic tradition, which is decidedly a lie.

Even when prizes and anthologies dedicated to Indigenous languages have the best of intentions, it strikes me that this segregation will only perpetuate the current situation: the possibility of publishing in languages other than Spanish are very few and far between, support for translation is scarce and the reading public in the original language is not very big. In general, the drive and presence of literary production in languages other than Spanish leaves much to be desired within the panorama of Mexican literature.

Indigenous literature does not exist. Literature exists in many different Indigenous languages. Different literary traditions exist in a great diversity of languages. Literature exists in Isthmus Zapotec, in Mixe, in Chontal, in Spanish, but a single Indigenous literature does not exist and if a Mexican literature exists it is by definition linguistically diverse.

I believe the movement to support literature in languages other than Spanish will be greatly enriched if publishers, festivals, fairs, bookshops and readers were to open up to the great diversity of languages and poetics that currently exists – all on the same level, all complex and equal. Though that might seem an impossible utopia, the state of things is gradually changing. The UNAM, for example, organises the Carlos Montemayor Languages of America Poetry Festival, where it's possible to hear creators in Zapotec, Portuguese and Mixtec speak in the same forum. Which should be the norm.

23 January, 2013

# HAHAHATL:
## NO LAUGHING MATTER?

A few months ago, my friend Guillermo de León (you can find him on the Tumblr blog 'De aquí y de allá') alerted me to a phenomenon occurring on social media, in which the suffix '-tl' is added to certain words so that they  'sound' like words in Nahuatl. Once I started exploring, I found some real gems, like the lovely word YOLOTL, which plays on YOLO, you only live once (a sort of carpe diem for twenty-first century social media) and the word yolotl (or yollotl) which means 'heart' in several Nahuan languages. As well as the excellent YOLOTL, I found other uses such as 'jajajatl', 'fiestatl'... and even the suffix '-tl' added to common phrases in English: 'I love youtl', 'Like a bosstl', for example.

This type of linguistic game is relatively common and emerges from the interaction between speakers of different languages. I've always been curious about the mechanisms that are activated when we select relevant patterns and apply them to our own language so it 'sounds' like another. To give the impression that they're speaking in French, Spanish-speaking Mexicans substitute the articles 'el' and 'la' for 'le' and put an acute accent on words: 'le perré' instead of 'el perro', the dog, or 'le niñé' instead of 'el niño', the boy. To do the same with Russian, the ending '-ozky' is usually added to words in Spanish: 'casozky' for 'casa', house, or 'mermeladozky' for 'mermelada', jam. The historian Sebastián van Doesburg told me how speakers of Dutch add the ending '-os' to give the impression they're speaking in Spanish. To play these games and make these inferences, a degree of language interaction is required. Who in Spanish could play a similar game with Swahili? What ending would we need to give the impression of speaking Swahili in Spanish? We wouldn't be able to decide on one because distance means that interaction between speakers barely exists. In Mixe, for example, I use the ending '-o' to give the impression I'm speaking in Spanish: 'wo'ojko' instead of 'wo'ojk', haircut, for example. In contrast, I use the ending '-ach (atsy)' to give the impression I'm speaking Mixe from the central region: 'wo'ojk'atsy' instead of 'wo'ojk'.

So far, you might think the use of the ending '-tl' is part of this phenomenon derived from language contact and from our impressions of certain characteristics that allow us to create word games in our own languages. However, the phenomenon isn't as simple as it looks. The first strange thing about the use of the ending '-tl' is that it isn't just used to make Spanish sound like Nahuatl, but to make it sound 'Indigenous', as though Indigenous languages were a single homogenous unit. This speaks volumes, because we're not talking about distant languages but rather languages that have coexisted with Spanish for centuries. In memes, the images accompanying phrases ending in '-tl' are of people who belong to various, very different, Indigenous communities. Why is the suffix '-tl' used to accompany an image of Rigoberta Menchú, a speaker of a Mayan language? The Mayan language family is completely different to the Uto-Aztecan family to which the Nahuan languages belong.

Despite centuries of coexistence, the users of these memes seem not to understand the profound linguistic differences between languages such as Mixtec, Tarahumara, Tzotzil and Nahuatl. It would be like using the ending '-ozky' for both Russian and Japanese just because they are both non-American languages. This particular example is unthinkable, yet it's predictable when it comes to languages known as Indigenous, despite the only thing they have in common being that they were spoken here before the arrival of Cortés. To take the idea even further, Nahuatl isn't even a single linguistic system, but rather, according to some specialists, more than fifteen mutually unintelligible languages. Not all Nahuan languages use the phoneme /tl/, so that ending is associated with only a subset of them.

So, all in all, this would seem to be a case of grave ignorance, but ignorance nonetheless. But the issue doesn't end there: what criteria are used to choose the images accompanying these phrases? Some of them were chosen because the people in them are wearing clothing that differs from typical western garb, but others not. I ask again, how do they know someone belongs to an Indigenous community and that their image is therefore eligible to accompany the phrase ending with '-tl'? Is there something to be said about skin colour here? If it's not clothing, then what's driving the choice of images in these memes? It seems obvious to me that the construction of the '-tl' memes is racist. It racialises Indigenous people and assigns them certain character-istics. It treats 'Indigenous' as a race and not as a political category in the context of colonisation; it categorises Indigenous people as an inferior and homogenous race. Because of the mere fact of inhabiting this territory before the arrival of Hernán Cortés, all Indigenous people constitute, in those memes, a single race with a certain skin colour who speak a single language: Nahuatl. They are also an inferior race, as can be deduced from the comments accompanying these memes. The use of the '-tl' ending goes from being just a word game to being, in these memes, a clear manifestation of racism.

*Indigenous is NOT a racial category. Repeat a thousand times.*

X                    *3 Sept, 2016*

*Indigenous people are _____*
*\*Whatever fills in the blank will almost certainly be an unsustainable generalisation.*

X                    *4 June, 2016*

Word games with these kinds of endings can be just that: word games arising from the interaction between several languages, but they always end up tied to prejudices and relationships between communities of speakers. There will be someone out there using the '-ozky' ending in certain contexts to characterise Russians as violent mafiosos. Not always, but it happens. The game itself is not the problem, but rather the context to which it belongs and in which it is used.

In an ideal world, speakers of Spanish, when playing these word games, would use an ending for a specific variety of Nahuatl, another for Mixe, another for Maya and so on for each language spoken in this country. But no, it could never be a simple word game in a context like

*Indigenous languages are modern languages too, you know.*

X                    *14 Nov, 2013*

ours. For the time being, I suggest you use the ending '-at' if you want your words to sound like Ayutla Mixe, my mother tongue.

One of the worst examples of this meme uses an image of two Ixil women testifying, during the trial of the

Guatemalan dictator Efraín Ríos Montt,  to the torture, rape and terrible massacre of the Ixil people by the Guatemalan army. Their testimony was an extraordinary act of bravery and dignity that ending up as a meme accompanied by the phrase 'Ta buena esta cumbiatl' – 'Not bad, this cumbiatl'. Truly shameful.[7]

28 Aug, 2015

---

[7]  This article is available on the *Este País* webpage: https://estepais. com/.

# You're so Splenda, I'm all panela...

𝕏 4 Dec, 2018

What language are you, according to your star sign?

Aries: Tapachultec
Taurus: Cree
Gemini: Guarijio
Cancer: Tepehua
Leo: Romani
Virgo: Cherokee
Libra: Swahili
Scorpio: Popoloca
Capricorn: Popoluca
Sagittarius: Mayo
Aquarius: Maya
Pisces: Huave

𝕏 24 Feb, 2015

You do know illiterate isn't an insult, right? Nobody goes around accusing people of not having mastered the oral tradition.

𝕏 24 Feb, 2015

Finishing off writing an essay while trying to make sure my turkeys don't escape, winning, as always.

🅕 31 Oct, 2011

¡¡Ja xëë tsontäknëp, jaa ja tetymyä̈äy täkmä̈äy jyënkonët!!

The party's about to get started – the grandparents are on their way...

**f** 21 Aug, 2016

Conversations with my grandmother:

Y:

So you see,
garlic isn't Mixe,
the Spanish
brought it over.

G:

That can't
be true!!!
What do you
mean it's
not Mixe!!!
That's not fair,
there's no way
our ancestors had
to eat without
garlic!!! It can't be
true, it must
be Mixe.

Y:

Well, it's not, but
think about it,
the Spanish
didn't have
avocados, for example.

G:

Ah well,
that evens things
out a bit.
Poor things.

(…I don't want to
be there when she
finds out the Oto-Mangueans
brought corn to the Mixe-Zoques,
I'm scared of how she might react).

**X** 1 Aug, 2018

There's a strong
relationship between
linguistic and biological
diversity: of the thirteen
countries with most
languages, twelve also
figure on the list of
countries with the greatest
diversity of biological
species.

---

**f** 2 April, 2016

You, me, staring into
each other's eyes in the
darkness of the forest,
lit only by billions of
fireflies. I don't know,
think about it…
#HighlandLove

# PART II:

## WHEN BRIDGES
## STOP BEING BUILT

# SLAVERY AND THE GENESIS OF CREOLE LANGUAGES

In even the worst conditions of slavery, violence and abuse, humans have had the ability to create and recreate the sophisticated mental constructions known as languages. So said Dr Michel Launey, specialist in classical Nahuatl and expert in the linguistic diversity of French Guyana, where creole languages are spoken alongside Indigenous languages and French, as they are in several countries in America. Many of these creole languages came into being in the context of slavery: when the languages of enslaved Africans transported to America came into contact with European languages, new linguistic systems were created.

It's hard to find evidence of the creation of languages, unless we believe the myth of Babel. We know that languages change over time and that their origins date back to the emergence of humanity. Languages evolve slowly so that, for example, ancient Oto-Manguean has become present day Ixcatec, just as ancient Latin became the Spanish spoken today in

> *You, me, ten thousand years ago, domesticating teosintle and turning it into corn, preparing kupiipy nä'äny and sharing it for the first time with humanity, I don't know, think about it...* *#MesoamericanLove*
>
>  *10 Oct, 2017*

Mexico City. The origins of languages go back thousands of years and accompanied *Homo* perhaps even before they became today's *Homo sapiens sapiens.*

It's hard to find proof of the emergence of languages, except in one case: creole languages offer us a privileged insight, allowing us to witness and study the birth of a new language. A creole language is an extraordinarily interesting linguistic phenomenon, but it's also a social phenomenon that's almost always linked to contexts of exploitation.

> *Language cannot be regulated; it self-regulates. Save yourself the effort.*
>
> X                4 Mar, 2014

Let's take a look at their gestation: sometimes, when communities or groups of humans with different languages come into contact, they create a simplified linguistic code, combining the lexis of one language with the grammar and structures of the other in order to establish communication with concrete ends. These codes are known as pidgins. Because there isn't enough time for the speakers of one language to learn the other group's language (or because conditions such as slavery impede it), elements of both linguistic systems mix in order to resolve the urgent and contextual need for communication. From this mixture, a new code is created, and so we witness the birth of what will later become a new language.

When this pidgin is learned by children as their first language, as their mother tongue, it acquires all the characteristics and complexities of any other language in the world: it's then that the pidgin becomes a creole language; a language emerging from the often violent meeting of two peoples with radically different languages. From distinct parents there emerges a new language which, as soon as it's born, takes an independent path, becoming a language in its own right. When a pidgin becomes a generation of children's first means of naming, thinking about, and communicating with the world, that pidgin acquires a birth certificate and is henceforth a complete, rich and complex language like all the rest: a creole language.

The Chabacano language emerged in the first half of the eighteenth century from contact between Tagalog and Spanish in the Philippines (see the YouTube video titled 'Chabacano Cavite ¿Comprendes criollo español de Filipinas?'); Palenquero,  currently spoken in Colombia, emerged from contact between speakers of Spanish and Portuguese and enslaved Africans, who spoke languages from the Bantu family and escaped slavery at the end of the sixteenth century; Sranan Tongo (spoken in Suriname) was created from contact between central and western African languages, Dutch, a little English and a bit of Portuguese (see the YouTube video 'Words of Life SRANAN TONGO (Sranan Tongo) People/Language Movie Trailer').

In addition to the dreadful history of their birth in the context of slavery, creole languages of the American continent continue to face linguistic prejudices and are often assumed to be corrupt mixtures. They're treated as 'degenerate Dutch' or 'outcast Spanish' or pejoratively described as 'Black people's English.' It's often said they're not distinct languages but just corrupt varieties of others. These words and labels often continue to wound the languages of descendants of Africans who, in the context of everyday violence, were able to create, in terrible, inhumane contexts, something beautiful, complex and entirely human: a new language.

16 Oct, 2013

# WHEN BRIDGES
# STOP BEING BUILT

There are many reasons why a person might decide to learn a language: I know someone who wanted to learn Russian so they could read the stories they'd read in Spanish as a child, someone else who learned Spanish so they could argue with the preachers insisting on converting them to a new religion, and another person who learned German so they could understand the lyrics of their husband's favourite songs. Behind the desire to learn a new language is always a desire to build bridges with others or with the world enjoyed through that language – to access articles published in Mandarin, sing songs in French, understand Japanese manga. One of the most powerful gestures of respect you can make to someone is to learn to speak their language; to expose yourself to laughter at your initial bad pronunciation and amusing errors, and to the discomfort of not immediately being able to access the vocabulary you need. We all know how good it feels when someone makes an effort to speak to us in our language. We appreciate the kindness of foreign language speakers who try and communicate with us in Spanish, but the same is rarely true of someone whose mother tongue is Tepehua, say, who has made considerable efforts to learn Spanish. And it's rarer still to find a Spanish speaker who's had the deference to learn Tepehua and tries to communicate in that language while on Tepehua land.

There are many reasons to learn a new language but there's only one reason to stop speaking one, especially if it is your mother tongue: discrimination against speakers of that language. A person who speaks English as their mother tongue, for example, doesn't try to stop speaking it once they've learned French and Spanish. No one in any normal circumstances tries to speak fewer languages. Why then does this happen in the case of Indigenous languages? Why is it common for someone who speaks Ayuujk as their mother tongue to try and stop speaking it once they've learned Spanish? Why is it common to find people who speak an Indigenous language and Spanish doing everything they can to ensure their children *aren't* bilingual? Why, if there are so many different languages in this country, don't we have sufficient deference to learn them? It's nothing to do with the languages themselves but with the way they're valued – a value that's entirely extra-linguistic, I should add. A native Spanish speaker living somewhere like Mexico City can learn new languages without needing

> Monolingual Mixe speaking grand-mother. Bilingual Mixe-Spanish speaking mother. Monolingual Spanish speaking granddaughter. Sound familiar?
>
> 03 Feb, 2016

> So now it turns out monolingualism in Mixtec is a terrible problem but monolingualism in French is not. The reasons for this are known as discrimination and colonialism.
>
> 4 Sept, 2013

> We shouldn't be talking about minority languages but about minor-itised languages.
>
> 5 Mar, 2017

to abandon their mother tongue, but that person is much more likely to want to stop speaking Spanish and learn English if they're living as an undocumented migrant in a city in the United States. The mother tongue is the same, but the circumstances are different. There are so many reasons to want to learn new languages, but only one to want to stop speaking them.

14 Dec, 2011

# CASSANDRA AND
# LANGUAGE DEATH

In one version of the story – because oral narratives are open texts with multiple pathways – the god Apollo spits in Cassandra's mouth after awarding her the gift of being able to see the future. In doing so he curses her, condemning her to the knowledge that no one will ever believe her. Despite knowing in advance what the future will bring, she is left desperate, unable to take the necessary measures to prevent the destruction of her city. In cases like Cassandra's, prior knowledge turns into useless despair.

Something similar is happening with the ongoing linguicide in Mexico and around the world. We know that never before in the history of humanity has language death reached these heights; we know that according to experts' calculations, in the next hundred years half of all languages will have disappeared; we know that every day the number of speakers of Mexican languages other than Spanish is diminishing.[8] We also know that this language death is the consequence of the systematic violation of specific communities and people. Even so, language policy in this country hasn't changed much, despite the

---

[8]    On this topic, see the following document: UNESCO, *Atlas of the World's Languages in Danger* (Paris, 2010).

existence of institutions and organisations promoting linguistic diversity. The basic factors required for language rights to be respected and for the construction of a society that respects and enjoys linguistic diversity haven't even been clearly set out yet. Yes, communities of speakers play a fundamental role in the task of keeping these languages alive, but the Mexican government also needs to respect people's language rights and reverse the process of Hispanicisation that was set so industriously in motion, so many years ago. This is not happening.

For starters, the Mexican state owes an apology to Indigenous communities and speakers of Indigenous languages for violating their fundamental language rights and for the physical, psychological and cultural ravages their 'Spanish-only' policy has inflicted. What follows will be hard work, work that's not being fully undertaken. Although language rights, which are also human rights, have been recognised, the necessary changes aren't being pursued with the same enthusiasm with which Hispanicisation was undertaken. The state education offered to speakers of Indigenous languages remains far from bilingual, and many teachers are located outside the relevant linguistic areas, so it's possible to find a Mixe-speaking teacher in a community of Chatino speakers or a Triqui-speaking teacher in a school where the children's mother tongue is Mixe. What do we have to do to make sure teachers in the education system aimed at Indigenous communities are, at the very least, placed in the right linguistic area? Another minimal requirement is that linguistic and cultural diversity should form an important part of the core curriculum in schools all over the country; we know this isn't the case

> *My patriotic glands are blocked, they're not secreting national pride hormones.*
>
>  8 Sept, 2017

because most Mexicans can't name the languages spoken in their own country, or else they refer to Indigenous languages as 'dialects'. What do we have to do to get the Ministry of Public Education to incorporate the teaching of linguistic diversity into core primary school learning materials?

The situation regarding language rights in the judicial system is far from ideal; there's still a serious lack of interpreters, and this constitutes a barrier to access to justice, a basic human right. On the other hand, language ability is still not considered an important requirement for administrative workers sent to territories where the population speaks a language other than Spanish. I've had interactions with civil registry officials in Mixe territory who do not speak Mixe, and with staff in the local public prosecutor's office who do not speak Zapotec. It would be strange, to say the least, to find a public servant who did not speak Portuguese in Brazil, say. Again, this is basic stuff.

We could go on, turning to various areas of government, to hospitals on Indigenous land that have no interpreters, information about social development programmes directed at speakers of Indigenous languages but only available in Spanish,

*Sometimes I feel that asking for something from the state is like asking your kidnapper, now that they've got you locked up, to please not be too hard on you. But then I remember that there's no alternative, at least for now – that the kidnapper uses our taxes to keep us locked up, and all we can do is ask them not to use those resources against us. Meanwhile, let's imagine a world not divided into those legal-political entities known as 'countries'. What would that world be like? How would it be organised? I'm under no illusion that I'll ever get the chance to live in a post-nation-state world, but let no one ever say I didn't dream about it.*

                    *23 Mar, 2017*

75

media coverage exclusively in Spanish, books in languages that aren't our mother tongue and so on, throughout all levels of government, a government stubbornly opposed to all common sense in continuing to be monolingual in Spanish even in different linguistic territories. This is a veiled extension of the Hispanicisation project. It's pointless to repeat that languages are dying, pointless to scream like Cassandra, because the Mexican state continues to Hispanicise in its everyday functions, even as it praises linguistic diversity in its laws and discourse.

20 Feb, 2015

# LET LANGUAGES DIE IN PEACE

In a context where diversity is increasingly valued, at least in public discourse, it seems foolish to ask whether linguistic diversity around the world should be protected or not.

And yet, among all the different voices, there is a school of thought arguing

> – *Many of the world's languages are dying.*
> – *Never mind, keep training linguistic specialists in the suffix -ku.*
> *Some people actually say stuff like this…*
>
> **f**                    *25 Nov, 2016*

that, faced with the accelerated loss of language diversity, languages should not be saved. According to this stance, that fact that half of the world's languages will have died out within a hundred years, as current estimates suggest, only goes to show that linguistic diversity is ceasing to be useful for humanity.

Among the arguments, which show varying levels of seriousness, those put forward by Kenan Malik in his article 'Let Them Die' centre on the fact that languages, being above all instruments in the service of human communication,  disappear when they cease to be useful to a community in their efforts to fulfil their communicative needs. In other words, Malik argues that the reason Mixe is dying is simply because its speakers prefer Spanish as a means of communication; Mixe has stopped being useful to them. In this sense, taking action to strengthen linguistic diversity would go against the people's right to choose which language they wish to use. Languages die because speakers decide they will, Kenan Malik seems to argue. From this perspective, the linguistic homogenisation of the world is desirable because it would help maximise communication between very different countries and cultures; seen this way, the Babel punishment does seem to be a real curse.

On the one hand, I agree with this stance insofar as the conservation and vitality of a language is directly linked to those who speak it; we cannot put the conservation of linguistic diversity above the quality of life of its speakers. However, what this stance seems to ignore is that when a language dies it isn't just simply because it ceases to be useful for communication within a community whose speakers have decided they prefer another language; what's missing from this argument is that a language becomes endangered in contexts where its speakers are discriminated against. The disappearance of languages doesn't happen suddenly and in a vacuum; the decision to stop speaking a language implies its speakers have long suffered discrimination. Nobody decides to stop speaking a language simply because another one strikes them as more useful.

*The personal is political? The linguistic is political — not just cultural, not folkloric, political!*

X        *30 July, 2014*

The loss of a language is not a peaceful process in which speakers abandon one language for another; it's a process in which its speakers are subjected to punishment, contempt and usually colonialism. Strengthening linguistic diversity isn't just about preserving languages as abstract entities; it's also about making sure speakers don't experience discrimination and, as a result, don't have to stop using their own language if they need or wish to learn another. Speakers of languages that don't provoke discrimination don't wish to stop speaking their own languages simply because they've learned to speak another, no matter how useful they consider it to be. Why should a Mixe person stop speaking their mother tongue just because they've learned to speak Spanish?

> *If you can speak Mixe with your mum or dad but not with your son or daughter, something has happened, something's going on, something's being snatched away from you, and there's something you can do about it…*
>
> 𝕏         *22 Dec, 2017*

3 April, 2013

# LINGUISTIC PARANOIAS

Discrimination towards Indigenous languages takes many forms. One head emerges, you chop it off and two more grow back. It needs to be cut off completely, the wounds cauterised. One way it materialises is the strange paranoia roused in some people when a Mexican language that isn't Spanish is used in front of them. 'It makes me feel like you're bitching about me the whole time,' someone told me once, before asking a friend and I to avoid speaking Mixe in their presence. I didn't quite know how to respond and asked myself if it was disrespectful to speak in another language in front of people who can't understand it. Is it? In what contexts? Under what circumstances? I stopped talking in Mixe in that person's presence until the day I realised they weren't perturbed in the slightest by two people holding long conversations in English.

This situation seems to be replicated in many ways in other spaces. Several Mixe women who are domestic workers told me they've had to deal with situations where they were forbidden from speaking their mother tongue in their place of work. Phone calls with friends were only permitted in Spanish. The argument was more or less the same: their employers felt that, somewhere among the words they couldn't understand, a plot was being woven against them. This situation shows that, among the many ways control can be exercised over another person, we must include control over the language in which they are allowed, or not allowed, to communicate. Where does the demand for courtesy end and the violation of language rights begin?

Another justification I've heard from Spanish-speaking teachers is that if pupils whisper in Mixtec the teachers won't understand the messages being exchanged. In this way, the demand to speak in Spanish becomes a way of combatting a specific paranoia that tends to apply more to Indigenous languages than generally to languages other than Spanish. I'd find it odd if, in my community, someone monolingual in Mixe were to demand that two people from another city stopped speaking in Spanish out of fear they were criticising what the Mixe speaker was wearing. Maybe it's normal to feel discomfited by two people speaking an unknown language that might allow them to keep secrets and exclude others. What's not normal is that speakers of Spanish can forbid speakers of Indigenous languages from doing it, but to do it the other way round would be strange. Perhaps it's discourteous to use a language that excludes others, but the difference lies in the power relations that allow speakers of one language to forbid that 'discourtesy' to the speakers of another, but not vice versa.

*In Mexico RACISM is pronounced MESTIZAJE.*

𝐟            *17 Sept, 2016*

The ideal thing would be to free us all. For there to be no Spanish speakers suffering from paranoia and no Indigenous language speakers scared of causing offence when using their language in front of others. The ideal thing would be to live in an environment where we can start listening to linguistic diversity without worrying about controlling what others might be saying about us; in any case, we're probably not important enough to be the focus of a conversation between two people speaking a Mexican language that isn't our own.

4 Dec, 2013

# TEST: ARE YOU PREJUDICED AGAINST INDIGENOUS LANGUAGES?

## PART I

Although these days politically correct discourse always includes praise for multiculturalism and multilingualism, prejudices that work against language equality can still be found crouching behind our attitudes and tangled up in our opinions. Many of us perhaps know that languages all have the same value and that, as linguistic systems, they are equally complex and equally effective for communication. We might also be conscious that discrimination against languages has direct repercussions for their vitality. Despite all this, it appears few people, given the choice, would send their children to Nahuatl rather than German lessons. Combating our own prejudices also implies taking appropriate action; changing our prejudices involves changing our attitude and those changes always free and enrich us.

The first step, as always, is to be conscious of each prejudice. What follows is a list describing certain phrases that discriminate against Indigenous languages, by way of a kind of guide to reflecting on our own beliefs and attitudes that, at the end of the day, influence the way we value Mexican languages and their vitality.

1.  'Our dialects sound so lovely, don't they!' I heard this phrase on a public TV programme that airs on Saturdays. Since the channel has a decent audience, you'd hope the station's discourse might be – how shall I put it? – better informed. We have to keep insisting, repeating until we're blue in the face, that language equality begins with how we name them, and that Indigenous  languages are not dialects and therefore should not be named as such. This prejudice seems to be very recent; according to Michael Swanton, throughout the colonial period and right up to the end of the nineteenth century, Indigenous languages were called 'lenguas' or 'idiomas' – languages – never 'dialectos' in its pejorative sense.

2.  'Wait, Mixe can be written?' Yes, it can, and people have been doing it for more than 1,500 years. There are written records of Epi-Olmec, one of the ancestors of today's Mixe-Zoque languages. You hear all the time that Indigenous languages are oral languages that have only recently been written down using the Latin alphabet. Written words are thought of as sacred and writing seems to give languages permission to be modern.

    Yes, the oral tradition is important for Indigenous languages, but it's also crucial for all languages spoken today. What's more, since

86

Mesoamerica is one of the parts of the world where writing first emerged, we can hardly say that a language lacks a written tradition just because it's Indigenous. There is evidence of writing on stone, on codices, and a long colonial tradition in the Latin script that dwindled and almost disappeared with Independence, when the government stopped accepting Indigenous language texts. Now they're starting to be written again, in many cases continuing a tradition that was interrupted and which speakers have also forgotten (see the YouTube video 'El Coloquio de Lenguas Otomangues en Oaxaca. Conversación con Michael Swanton.flv' as well as 'El Valor de los Textos Escritos en Lenguas Indígenas – Michel Oudijk.flv').

There are even languages such as Isthmus Zapotec that had important publications throughout the whole of the twentieth century. According to Sebastián van Doesburg, 'writing in Zapotec has an almost uninterrupted written tradition dating back to 500 BC'. So we cannot maintain the prejudice that Indigenous languages are only oral languages.

3. 'Spanish connects us to the whole universe,' according to Jaime Labastida, director of the Mexican Academy of Language.[9] Amerindian languages, in contrast, 'take us to the depths of our selves and make contact with our roots' (see

[9] Jaime Labastida was director of the Mexican Academy from February 2011 to February 2019.

the article titled 'Universo del español', published in *Revista de la Universidad de México* in March 2013).

This type of prejudice, however subtle it may seem, is really damaging. In extreme cases, Spanish is pitched as a universal language that allows us to talk about every possible topic and which can establish many cultural bridges, while Indigenous languages are presented as being restricted to local phenomena, to content belonging only to the culture in question and to establishing contact with our roots, whatever that means. Indigenous languages, like any living world language, can be as universal or local as they need to be; all languages can create a variety of strategies that allow them to discuss any kind of knowledge or to describe any reality. You can access all kinds of information in Indigenous languages – you can learn about German history in Triqui or describe nanoscience in Purépecha. If this doesn't happen very often, it's not because the Indigenous languages prohibit it, but because their use has been truncated and their existence challenged. Indigenous languages are not condemned to communicate 'only our myths, legends and customs', as someone once suggested to me.

> *Indigenous peoples aren't just roots, we're new shoots as well.*
>
> X                    *13 July, 2012*

Claims such as the one cited above have been used by the director of the Mexican Academy of Language to try and push for Spanish to be legally established as the country's official language. (The controversy surrounding this proposal is discussed in 'El español como lengua oficial: propuesta polémica', by Abida Ventura.)

4. 'Indigenous languages have no grammar.' We mustn't confuse grammar – the set of rules and principles that govern the functioning of a language – with the book that describes this function. Every language in the world has grammar because every language has a clear way of working and clear characteristics. The fact that there isn't a published book compiling and describing the functioning of every single world language says more about the scarcity of linguists than about the value of those languages. And besides, many linguists *have* done the work of describing how Indigenous languages function and have been publishing those studies since the colonial era. Back then, these books weren't called 'grammars' but rather 'arts' *(Art of the Mexican Language*, for example). In any case, if it's the publication of a grammar that matters, Michael Swanton points out that the first grammar to describe the workings of the Zapotec language was published eight years before the first grammar of English.

5. 'The problem is they don't speak Spanish and don't wear shoes.' Another of the most common linguistic prejudices, as seen in the article titled 'Comunidades de Oaxaca viven un drama por hablar solo en mazateco' (Communities in Oaxaca having a nightmare because they only speak Mazatec), written by Karina Avilés and published on 28 February, 2012 in *La Jornada*, is to establish a direct relationship between poverty and monolingualism in Indigenous languages.

Not speaking Spanish is at least in part depicted as the cause of backwardness in many Indigenous communities. Of course, being bilingual gives you an advantage over people who speak only one language, but we mustn't forget that most monolingual people in this country speak only Spanish without this being perceived as  a problem. On the other hand, most bilingual people speak an Indigenous language. Though many journalists and public servants might think it so, speaking Spanish is not the magic solution to these problems, and nor is it a great indicator of progress. We all have the right to be educated and literate in our mother tongue, to receive administrative and health services in it, to have access to media with content in that language; in sum, to have all the same rights as native speakers of Spanish, who are never forced to navigate the criminal justice system in, say, Russian. If this does not happen, it isn't because Indigenous languages are incapable of it, but because the use of Spanish has been imposed even in our own communities. Only in this context and only because of the effects of discrimination and the violation of basic linguistic rights on our own land can it be claimed that speaking Spanish is better than speaking Mixtec.

*To be guaranteed a Mixe interpreter during a trial is not an advantage; it's to make up for the fact that the judicial system is monolingual.*

                15 Nov, 2014

To be continued…

18 Sept, 2013

# TEST: ARE YOU PREJUDICED AGAINST INDIGENOUS LANGUAGES?

## PART II

Let's continue our exploration of prejudices against Indigenous languages. Rather than trying to catch people out, the idea is to examine hidden beliefs that emerge unexpectedly in our speech and attitudes.

6. 'Our Indigenous languages are ancient.' In attempts to highlight the value of Indigenous languages, allies often come out with positive prejudices. It is said, almost always with good intentions, that Indigenous languages are much older than other languages. While languages such as German, English or French receive the label 'modern languages', Indigenous languages are 'ancestral' – they safeguard ancient knowledge. Is it true that Indigenous languages are ancestral? Yes, but not only Indigenous languages – rather, all living world languages are ancient. Every world language is derived from other languages

that changed little by little, generation after generation, until they became what they are today. Two thousand years ago 'Spanish' existed, only it was very different to the Spanish of today, so different that it was called Latin. It changed enormously over time, as it arrived in the Iberian Peninsula and then in America, so in some sense we can say that the Spanish spoken here today is a twenty-first century Latin unique to Mexico. What we now know as Spanish didn't emerge in a vacuum; it's the result of thousands of years of language evolution. The same can be said of Ayuujk: two thousand years ago, somewhere in the heart of Mesoamerica, people spoke a language very different to today's Mixe languages, one that changed so much that over time it became my mother tongue, Ayuujk. Spanish and Mixe are equally ancient, and so to describe only Indigenous languages in this way only exaggerates a difference that doesn't exist.

7. 'Indigenous languages are so hard to learn.' This phrase will discourage even the most enthusiastic, but an Indigenous language is not intrinsically harder to learn than any other. There are many factors that mediate our perception of complexity when it comes to language learning. Indigenous languages in Mexico belong to eleven separate linguistic families, and therefore represent immense variety. There are tonal languages such as the Oto-Manguean languages, agglutinative languages such as Nahuan languages or Purépecha, languages with complex vocalic systems such as the Mixe languages, or with impressive syllabic patterns, as Elena Ibáñez's studies of the Yuman language Paipai have shown. All these languages

can present difficulties, but that depends in large part on your mother tongue. The Spanish subjunctive tends to be a headache for native speakers of English. Indigenous languages are as difficult or easy to learn as other languages of the world, it just depends on who's learning them.

8. 'Indigenous languages are inherently poetic.' This is the classic positive prejudice against Indigenous languages. Well-intentioned in principle, it tends to be repeated when discussing intrinsic poetic value, based always on literal translations into Spanish in which a common word such as 'jotkujk' ('happy' in Ayuujk) is translated into Spanish literally as 'to have one's entrails straightened out', giving it a poetic effect it did not originally possess. This prejudice tends to be found mainly in literary publications. The truth is that Indigenous languages are not naturally poetic; they can be as prosaic as any other

*So many twists and turns, over so many years, only to conclude what we knew all along: that the poetic function of language in the West cannot be separated from the birth of music. Let's not forget, then, that when it emerged poetry was closer to music than it was to writing. Let's not forget, then, that literature is only one of many manifestations of that universal function of language: the poetic function. Not everything poetic needs to be written down. Imagine if one day they gave the Nobel Prize in Literature to a community of speakers for their poetic oral tradition? It couldn't be called the Nobel Prize in Literature anymore, but rather the Nobel Prize in the Poetic Function of World Languages. By awarding it to Dylan they're one step closer to making this name change a reality.*

❶ *13 Dec, 2016*

93

language in the world, as well as rude, ordinary or sublime. Depending on the context, we can use poetic or common, plain, everyday language.

9. 'But you don't even have an accent!' This is one of the phrases I've heard most often by way of praise. 'Seriously? You speak an Indigenous language? I didn't know, you can hardly hear the accent.' The assumption that all speakers of Indigenous languages will speak Spanish with a certain 'accent' reveals poor knowledge of the process of second language acquisition. Just like people who learn English as a second language, there will be some people who speak it with a more noticeable accent than others. This has to do with many factors; for example, someone who spends more time listening to and speaking English as a second language will have greater skill in that language than someone who only uses it once in a while or when the need arises. My grandmother rarely needs to use Spanish to live a full life – to carry out the activities she most enjoys – and her skills in Spanish are sufficient for her to be able to interact whenever she needs to. Speaking an Indigenous language does not remotely interfere with one's ability to learn Spanish or any other language.

> *There are people who think that when Indigenous people learn Spanish we all end up talking like Pedro Infante playing the 'Indian' in Tizoc…*
>
> ●        *23 Aug, 2012*

I'll draw our test to a close here. All that remains is to reflect and act on the results, so we can enjoy language diversity: it's hard to enrich yourself with or take enjoyment from something that's looked down on. Negation and discrimination are damaging to both sides – damaging to the discriminated languages and damaging to the discriminating parties who, by looking down on them, deny themselves knowledge and experiences that are there for the taking. Can you think of any other prejudices against Indigenous languages?

25 Sept, 2013

# BORDERS, WHY BORDERS?

'¿Fronteras? ¿Por qué fronteras? Si en mi música hay amor' – *Borders? Why borders? When in my music there's love* – sang the Argentine Leo Dan in one of his best-known songs. Something similar could be said of languages and borders between countries. Thanks to the patently absurd idea that each country must correspond to a single identity and a single language, Indigenous communities' own borders and linguistic areas were never taken into account when nation states were formed.

If we examine the political division of our country, the situation speaks for itself. Neither internal nor external borders respect the limits of communities and languages. Division by municipality is one example. In Oaxaca, for example, it's common for community authorities to also be municipal authorities; municipalities are governed by the Indigenous peoples themselves, which is to say, a state entity (the municipality) often coincides with an entity belonging to the Indigenous people in question: the community. However, though this situation is common in Oaxaca (unlike in other states, where municipal capitals are not governed by Indigenous populations), it doesn't mean municipal borders have taken linguistic borders into account. Within any given municipality you might find radically different communities with significant linguistic differences. In other Mexican states, the situation is worse; Indigenous communities almost always have to answer to councils or municipal heads who aren't Indigenous. In these cases, the municipal entity doesn't coincide with the relevant unit, the Indigenous community, and therefore nor with linguistic borders.

The division into federal entities tells us even more; Mixtec languages are spoken across three states: Oaxaca, Puebla and Guerrero. What would have happened if all the Mixtec languages and Mixtec peoples had formed their own single territory or state? What would happen if that linguistic area were contained within a single state? It would be interesting to see what the impact would be on the vitality or strength of those languages. As with municipalities, division into federal entities doesn't obey linguistic borders, meaning that speech communities and Indigenous peoples are divided by borders created by the Mexican state.

Mexico's external borders also divided Indigenous peoples, with even more serious consequences. We must remember, too, that the country's borders have changed many times, going right back to the colonial era, but that at no point were original peoples' own territorial limits respected.

*Nation states are to linguistic diversity what water is to oil.*

X                    12 Jan, 2015

The Yuman peoples and the Cocopah people were divided by the border between the United States and Mexico. The division between peoples wasn't respected to the south, either; the Chuj and Mam languages have speakers on both sides of the Mexico–Guatemala border. In addition, thanks to the displacement resulting from the civil war in Guatemala, there are communities in Mexico that speak other Guatemalan languages. Given this context of migration, according to certain friends of mine, it's common for Mexican Chuj speakers to suffer the same treatment as their fellow Guatemalans, being forced to prove their nationality when travelling to the country's interior. They are a single people divided by a border that no one ever asked them about.

That said, I don't think borders matter so much when communities decide to work together. But it remains the case that no geopolitical division, whether between municipalities, states or countries, coincides with Indigenous peoples' territories and linguistic areas. Does this have consequences? What are they?

*Mapuche nation divided between two states: Argentina and Chile.*

X                    *25 Sept, 2017*

*Sami nation divided among four states: Sweden, Norway, Finland and Russia.*

X                    *25 Sept, 2017*

*Cocopah nation divided between two states: Mexico and the United States.*

X                    *25 Sept, 2017*

19 June, 2013

# ON CHAIROS, THE LEFT AND INDIGENOUS PEOPLE

'And then, like a good chairo, he wanted to take Nahuatl lessons', I heard in a metro carriage a few months ago. From the way it's used in various contexts, we can surmise that the term 'chairo' describes people who identify with leftist ideas and often with the movement to respect Indigenous peoples' rights, even though they themselves are not Indigenous. The comment on the metro made me think about that movement's highlights and lowlights, its ideas, and who is involved or interested in the process of recognising original peoples' rights. It's true that people sympathetic to the causes of Indigenous communities have made enormous contributions to the Indigenous movement; I know a great many people who have established healthy, supportive and respectful relationships with the country's various cultures. The contributions made by certain thinkers, anthropologists and social activists have been invaluable (although others have been indifferent or even harmful). Linguists who have studied the languages spoken around the country

> *Indigenism and the Indigenous movement are two very, very different things — contradictory things, even.*
>
>  *12 April, 2017*

carry out crucial work that can have a direct impact on the strength of those languages. There are people who have crossed the bridge and learned our languages, who have taken on the challenge of living immersed in another culture, who have not just analysed the way we live but also spent time with us and adopted our ways.

> *Mexico is a plurinational state, not a multicultural one – two very, very different things.*
>
> 𝕏        *12 Aug, 2018*

Which is exactly what original peoples do, every day, although in their case it's considered much less extraordinary.

It is impossible to explain many of the Indigenous movement's achievements without the solidarity of people and initiatives which, over many years, contributed to the cause and understood that nation-building should involve recognising all of the many nations involved: each with their own story and language, with their own identity and particular way of life.

That said, the dark side of this is that there are other people and movements who, though they might claim to be sympathetic, have done more harm than good for the recognition of native languages and cultures. It strikes me that their expressions of sympathy actually hide a profound ignorance. Folklore is one great example: an easy, comfortable way of relating to other cultures without having to reflect on their artistic creations; all it takes is a spectacle to confirm prejudices about how 'multicoloured and celebratory' the Indigenous world is. Folklore is a consumer product and so will never give the spectator a real image, only ever a prefabricated one.

Another damaging approach perpetuates the myth of the noble savage. Idealising original peoples only ends up simplifying our ways of life. One of the most subtle ways of discriminating against the other is to deny them the ability to err; to fail to recognise that they are as complex as any other human. This kind of discrimination is more subtle than when based on skin colour or the shape of one's nose, attitudes that can at least be tackled head on; on the contrary, this kind of discrimination is disguised as sympathy and solidarity. Indigenous people are as good, bad, complex and human as anyone else.

Another vision, which I'll refer to as New Age, has also done terrible damage. Our relationship with nature is often more complex than in other cultures, but this is not the case for all original peoples. Not everything rural is Indigenous and not everything Indigenous is rural. It infuriates me how so many sympathisers with the Indigenous movement use our rituals and supposed methods of healing without remotely understanding them. It makes me angry when they use the word Pachamama – again, without understanding what it means. You can't reduce our

*Since it's almost my birthday, forgive me for throwing a bit of a tantrum. I can't stand Indigenous 'myth-busters' who say things like: 'Eek, I just found out something dreadful, did you know there are Indigenous communities that commit human rights violations?' I can't stand them, because they imply the belief that we are noble savages, which is incredibly offensive, because it denies me the right to wrongdoing and immediately calls on the Mexican government to do something – as if the government itself weren't one of the greatest human rights violators out there. The violation of human rights is, unfortunately, transcultural, and the fight against it should be too. Many Ayuujk people commit abuses and many others are angry about abuses committed in our community, just as we're angry about Guantanamo or about the death penalty in the United States. Should western culture be allowed to police other cultures? The struggle should be transcultural – that's what we're working towards...*

                              *15 Oct, 2012*

original peoples' culture to copal 'cleansing' ceremonies or psychedelic mushroom trips. Our languages aren't all poetry and music. It's unimaginably more complex than that.

It's a shame that most people who become interested in Indigenous peoples do so through folklore, or by idealising or caricaturising our cultures, varied as they are. I believe it's these representations that have prevented the rest of the non-Indigenous Mexican population from taking an interest in original peoples; it's because of these representations that attempts to learn Nahuatl are dismissed as being only for 'chairos'. A friend confessed to me that every time someone starts talking about the Indigenous world they can almost predict how the discussion will go, so they prefer to tune out of the conversation. The Indigenous movement is neither left-leaning or right-leaning – that division is alien to us; it's a struggle for the recognition of our rights and to establish healthy, equal intercultural relations. Folklore and idealisation are nothing but harmful to this process and, in truth, we could do without those kinds of sympathies.

Indigenous people and the Indigenous movement would prefer to have other sympathisers, not just urban healers who predict the end of the world based – supposedly – on the Maya calendar, or people looking for psychedelic trips or idealising our relationship with the sacred and with nature. We'd rather have critical, unprejudiced sympathisers, willing to get to know their country's other cultures and languages and how they too can shape and enrich us. We'd rather that a teenager in a technical

*OK, but seriously now… what are we going to do about that sad, inexplicable gulf between the Indigenous movement and Indigenous communities?*

                    *9 Feb, 2016*

college, an anthropologist from the National Institute for Anthropology and History, an expert in Norwegian industrial design, a contemporary art curator or a Joy Division fan could decide one day that it was just as worth their while to sign up to Nahuatl classes. That would be a good fresh start.

8 Aug, 2012

# AYUUJK: ALL BECAUSE THEY DIDN'T SPEAK SPANISH

## NEWSPAPER REPORTING ON LINGUISTIC DISCRIMINATION

It's widely known that speakers of Indigenous languages are constantly having their linguistic rights violated. This happens most often in the justice, health and education systems. The press has gradually started covering stories that involve linguistic discrimination; that said, I think it's important to consider the narratives and implications of approaches to the complex phenomenon that is the neglect of and often open discrimination against Indigenous language speakers.

News reports often outline terrible injustices suffered by people belonging to Indigenous communities who speak a Mexican language other than Spanish. The headlines of these articles tend to be along the following lines:

- 'Judge denies benefits to daughter of Indigenous mother who cannot speak Spanish' (Patricia Xicoténcatl, *Excélsior*, 8 March, 2015).

- 'Indigenous woman Marcelina Mejía condemned to 30 years in prison because she cannot speak Spanish' (Elisa Ruiz Hernández, *Página 3*, 28 July, 2015).

- 'Locked up for seven years in Chiapas because she couldn't say, "I didn't kill my son" in Spanish' (Inés Santaeulalia, *El País*, 20 March, 2012).

- 'University in Chiapas de-registers Indigenous student for not speaking Spanish' (*Sin Embargo*, 17 July, 2015).

This method of headlining news stories is notable because it's largely homogenous and because it centres on the problem of not speaking Spanish; it presents the fact of not speaking Castilian as a lack, a problem afflicting speakers of other Mexican languages. Monolingualism in Spanish is not depicted as a problem, but monolingualism in Indigenous languages repeatedly is. Even bilingualism in Indigenous languages is, in this context, a problem, while monolingualism in Spanish is not. You could speak Mixtec, Nahuatl and Cuicatec and it would make no difference; if you don't speak Spanish, you have a serious flaw.

It's not the monolingual speakers of Indigenous

*Remember Kafka's novel,* The Trial, *in which Josef K. never figures out what he's being tried for?? Adela García is a Mazatecan woman who's been in prison for eight years. She had no translator during her trial. This is not fiction, it's Mexico. How many cases like hers are there, cases that show us what Mexican justice is really like? Check out the defence work Cepiadet is doing in these kinds of cases. Today at 8pm on #LaRaízDoble on Canal 22 with Mardonio Carballo.*

*11 Oct, 2016*

languages who are violating linguistic rights. The problem isn't monolingualism, because if it were, monolingualism in Spanish would be depicted as a serious and undesirable condition afflicting most of the Mexican population.

The root of the problem is that the Mexican state and its entire administrative and institutional apparatus operates as a monolingual Spanish system incapable of tackling the challenges posed by a multilingual society. Even in the colonial period the country was better managed.

Let's carry out an exercise in rewriting: 'Judge who cannot speak Chontal denies benefits to Indigenous woman's daughter.' Thus the problem is shifted to the public servant who has not learned the language of the community in which she is working. 'Because he was not assigned an interpreter, Indigenous man Marcelino Mejía was condemned to thirty years in prison', emphasising the fact that most people who go through the criminal justice system do not have appropriate interpreters, as is their right and the state's obligation to provide. 'University in Chiapas deregisters Indigenous student because they could not offer education in his language', focusing on the fact that public universities *could* provide education in different languages, as would be natural in a truly multilingual country. 'Indigenous man condemned without evidence to thirty years in prison; he could not defend himself because neither his lawyer nor the judge speaks his mother tongue', highlighting the fact that there are no public defenders who speak the languages of the jurisdictions in which they work.

Most judges who operate in Mixe territory either do not speak the language or claim not to. It would be unthinkable to go to another country to work in education, health or the justice system without speaking the local language. And yet, this is common in Indigenous

*For that matter, all universities in Mexico ought to be intercultural...*

✕                    *28 June, 2012*

*Errata:*
*1. For 'On arriving in the community he was faced with the problem of the children not speaking Spanish', read...*

✕                    *27 Feb, 2014*

*2. 'On arriving in the community he was faced with the problem that he did not speak the children's mother tongue.'*

✕                    *27 Feb, 2014*

peoples' territories: judges, teachers and civil servants on, say, Mixtec land, but who do not speak Mixtec. We are not the problem. If we wanted, we could decide never to learn Spanish, but that doesn't mean our linguistic rights should be violated.

I think it's important to change the narrative and focus of news stories covering these cases. In many of these reports, the languages spoken by the people suffering these injustices are not even mentioned; it is as though the only thing that matters is that they don't speak Spanish. The way they're depicted in the press reinforces the idea that not speaking Spanish is a deficiency, while it doesn't matter if we don't speak Nahuatl or Mixe. Why? Our languages are legally Mexican. The fault is not ours. The problem is not that we don't speak Spanish, it's that the government refuses to see the evidence and operates, stubbornly, as though the country were monolingual. This is far from being the reality. And this story, too, deserves to be told.

16 Sept, 2015

# INDIGENOUS EDUCATION
# IN SPANISH?

*For Genaro Gil, who taught me to read. In memoriam.*

I learned to read Spanish before I learned to speak it. Or perhaps I should say I learned to decode the phonetic values associated with the set of letters that made up each word. I read aloud – fluently, even. Sometimes a word would rise up before me like an island full of meaning and, sometimes, by inferring from these islands, I could get an idea of the content of the text. The rest was a sonorous sea I didn't understand. I liked the sound of Spanish and I still remember many stories, tongue twisters and poems that I learned by heart to make my teachers believe they had successfully taught

> *Tsapajkx pëjy*
> *Ookänëp näjty, näjxnëp näjty.*
> *Tëë te'n a pä'äm myatäkn. Tëë*
> *te'n ja xëë ja et nëwä'äk, jaay ja*
> *jujky'äjtën kyëjxn. Aya'aky ja*
> *wyeen y'atujkn: tu'uk tsapajkx*
> *pëjy ojts t'ejxpääty, majtsk*
> *tsapajkx pëjy, tëkëëk, maktäxk,*
> *mëkoxk, e'px tsapajkx pëjy*
> *pyëjt tsujnaxy. Të'kxtëp, apëjpä-*
> *jktëp, ka'ookyëm tsyujët. Ojts ja*
> *änmëjä'än jatu'uk'oojky yakxon-*
> *ta'aky. Tu'ukety tu'ukety ojts*
> *jatëkoojk aya pye'tsnët: e'px,*
> *mëkoxk, tëkëëk, tu'uk. Ta ja*
> *yëjk'äjtën tu'ukteny myatäkn.*

 *1 Sept, 2016*

111

me to read. My mother, who didn't start learning Spanish until after she'd finished primary school, was known as early as Year 1 for having impeccable handwriting and spelling. I wasn't taught to write in my mother tongue; it wasn't until I was about twenty that I learned to read and write in Ayuujk.

Since the emergence of the idea of Mexico as a nation, the nascent country's unity, fragile as it was, was sustained principally by the idea of equality, or at least such was the discourse: no more castes, no more mestizos, criollos or 'saltapatrás' (a name referring to a perceived racial 'leap backwards'), no more zambos (children of an Indigenous person and a Black person) or indios – now everyone would be Mexican citizens and, as such, everyone should speak a single language and build a single history; they should have a single identity, a Mexican identity, whatever that may mean. The language of the new nation, though now free of the metropolis, was, paradoxically, the language of the metropolis. The existence of Indigenous languages began to be seen as a threat to the country's linguistic unity, and so Hispanicisation began in earnest, a Promethean gesture through which the torch that would put an end to the linguistic darkness of Indigenous peoples was raised.

This gave rise to absurd situations in classrooms. Let's imagine, for example, several Spanish-speaking children, who live in Mexico City in a Spanish-speaking social and family context, go to school for the first time. Their teachers, instead of *teaching* them to speak English, simply begin to talk to them and to expect them to read and write in English. What's more, they try to get the children to understand the

> *Because studying shouldn't have to involve leaving the countryside and leaving the countryside shouldn't mean 'bettering yourself'.*
>
> 15 Oct, 2017

112

differences between a subject and a direct object, between mammals, birds, fish and reptiles, or between adding and subtracting, by addressing them in a language nobody has ever taught them to speak before. So when the national exams come round it will be reported that these children have the worst level of education in the whole country. The conclusion is clear: the problem is that these children speak Spanish, which they should stop doing and instead speak exclusively in English. It occurs to almost no one that perhaps the problem is that the teachers were never trained to teach English as a second language, and that this might have been a good idea before they started on fractions, square roots or natural sciences.

This is what happens with Indigenous languages; it's that absurd. They try to teach us in a language we do not speak. Our low performance in educational evaluations has nothing to do with the fact that the children are Indigenous and everything to do with the state's inability to provide education that uses the children's languages as the medium of instruction; it's to do with the inability or lack of willingness to train teachers to teach Spanish as a second language in such a way that the children would receive a truly bilingual education. However, as far as education is concerned, the problem has been the very existence of linguistic diversity in the country and not the absurd way it has been tackled.

As a counterweight to the enthusiasm for Hispanicisation, a system of Indigenous education was later created, with bilingual schools that supposedly respect the children's mother tongues.

> *Now that's not fair, not all the SEP's[1] linguistic planning has turned out dreadfully. There's the Hispanicisation policy, that was crazy successful!*
>
> X                    *24 April, 2013*

---

[10]   Secretaría de Educación Pública (Ministry of Public Education).

However, their current functioning leaves much to be desired; it's common for the teachers, though they might fulfil the requirement of speaking an Indigenous language, to be assigned to a population that speaks a different one. In the best of cases, even if the teacher speaks the same language as the children, they have still never been trained to teach Spanish as a second language, and they only use the Indigenous language until the children are 'Hispanicised'. In my experience, the use of the Indigenous language is usually limited to a class in which they teach you to write a few words in Ayuujk. This is what passes for a bilingual Indigenous school in Mexico. Indigenous languages are almost never used as languages of instruction, as though it were impossible to take a class on evolution or Mexican history in Ayuujk.

I sometimes try to think of some advantage to having been taught to read and write in Spanish rather than in my mother tongue. I can't think of many, but I do have one favourite: the peculiar feeling as the phonetic structure of texts I'd learned by heart in childhood was gradually illuminated with meaning as I learned; those islands of meaning would grow and grow until one day, with an explosion of joy – sometimes at unhelpful moments (on the Mexico City metro or half-way through a conversation about the weather) – I'd suddenly fully understand that ocean of sound, the full meaning of the Quevedo poems I had long treasured in my mind. Their meanings were finally revealed to me. I think my sister is perhaps the only one who has ever understood this particular enthusiasm – understood it just as it is, without the need for further explanation.

18 April, 2012

# THE MEANINGS OF PAIN AND LINGUISTIC DIVERSITY

Pain is, almost by definition, a solitary experience. When we talk about pain, there is no way to be completely sure we're referring to exactly the same sensation as somebody else. How can we know that when I say 'it's throbbing' I mean the same as when you say 'it's throbbing'? What if my 'it's throbbing' corresponds to your 'it's stinging'? How do we know we're talking about the same thing when we talk about our pain? It's possible that pain and all the other bodily sensations we experience vary enormously from individual to individual, whether we group them under an 'it hurts', 'it throbs', 'it stings' or not. Without feeling the sensations of someone else's body we can never be sure. And yet, language allows us to give those sensations common names.

In Mixe, for example, I have a set of words to name physical pain: pëjkp, jäjp, pä'mp, we'tsp… I struggle to find equivalents for even one of these in Spanish. The differences are too great and there are moments when I can only describe a certain pain in Spanish or can only name it in Mixe. Knowing both languages means I have a richer inventory of words on the tip of my tongue to describe my pain, although in general, when something really hurts, Mixe takes over my thinking.

Communicating pain, especially when we're suffering and looking for relief, can be an exasperating experience. The problem is complicated further when it has to be done in a language radically different from your own and which you do not speak. Things go from bad to worse when you find yourself in a hospital with doctors whose understanding of the body, illness and pain is radically different to yours. And the problem can take on tragic dimensions when it comes to making a diagnosis.

How can we talk of fair access to health services when most hospitals that receive speakers of Indigenous languages don't have adequate translation and interpreting services? It is not only necessary to have bilingual staff, but also to have people who are trained to move from one system of understanding the body, health and pain to another, completely different system. Without those interpreters, it's impossible to guarantee the right to access to those health systems or to avoid potentially fatal misdiagnoses. Without those interpreters, there's no way of building bridges of empathy or of understanding whether your 'it hurts' is indeed the same as mine.

8 Jan, 2014

# A PSYCHOLOGICAL AND SOCIAL EXPERIMENT:

# LA CASA DEL ESTUDIANTE INDÍGENA

Multiculturalism always appears opposed to the idea of a nation, a single state or a single country. An under-standing of the construction of Mexico as an entity with a single coherent identity and a set of symbols that artic-ulate its inhabitants' thinking clashes with the existence of peoples that differ from one another, peoples with unique histories, with very different languages, and with complex identities. Neither Moctezuma's headdress, nor a mariachi band, nor the Huapango de Moncayo nor the china poblana can erase that fact. Multiculturalism denies the idea of the nation as it was originally imagined by those who declared its existence.

For Mexico to be possible, it was necessary for everyone to speak a single language, to develop a single identity and even to practise the same religion. Following that logic, the state launched a full-on battle against linguistic and cultural diversity. After two hundred years of independence, this is the result: though the discourse has changed, we are, right now, seeing the effects of those nationalist policies against particularities: languages are becoming extinct and cultural and linguistic diversity are under threat. Languages are dying at an unprecedented, almost unstoppable speed. There is no denying that this situation is a direct consequence of the obsession with nation building. We have sacrificed Mexico in favour of creating the idea of Mexico.

As part of this obsession with erasing differences, the Mexican government undertook integration projects that had varying levels of success but which almost without exception had catastrophic consequences for the subjects of that integration. In 1925, Plutarco Elías Calles opened the Casa del Estudiante Indígena (Indigenous Students' House) in Mexico City, a 'wonderful psychological and social experiment' in the words of the then Education Secretary himself.[11] To carry out this project, a group of 'pure Indians' was gathered and taken to Mexico City to live in the Casa. The goal was to civilise them; to transform their mentality, their habits and customs so that, once returned to their communities, they could be agents

> *Discriminate against you because of your skin colour? Let me be clear: the fact that races don't exist as biological categories doesn't mean they don't exist as social and ideological categories. RACES DO EXIST. They operate and structure, creating privilege and oppression. Essentially, they maintain the racist system. One of racism's main successes is to make us believe that races exist as biological categories – it's to have disguised itself as a scientific category.*
>
> 𝕏                    *23 Sept, 2016*

---

[11] For more on this exchange, see E. Loyo (1996), 'La empresa redentora: La Casa del Estudiante Indígena', *Historia Mexicana* 46: 99–131 (also cited by Yásnaya at the end of this essay), from which the words of then Education Secretary José Manuel Puig Casaurac are taken.

of assimilation who would integrate their communities into a monocultural nation that was monolingual in Spanish. What's more, the Casa del Estudiante Indígena aimed to demonstrate that the students could achieve the same level of intelligence as the rest of the population who did not speak an Indigenous language.

To fill the Casa, municipal governors and presidents were asked to send 'pure blood Indians', some of whom were practically abducted in order to fulfil the quota. Despite interest from the country's president, the accommodation was terrible and over time the house suffered hugely from neglect and fell into disrepair, to the extent that the quality of life of the pupils was seriously affected. They often lacked water for their basic needs and the sanitary conditions were deplorable. The initial scholarship awarded them by the SEP was quickly suspended. Many died of disease or else escaped. On top of all this, the pupils in the house were treated like animals in an experiment: their physical proportions were measured and they were made to undergo psychological tests to determine whether they were 'pure blood Indians' and to demonstrate that they were no less intelligent than pupils from the city.

As well as living in these conditions, the pupils described suffering serious psychological damage as a result of being brought from their communities to be 'civilised' in a completely different context. They would never come to belong to this new context but at the same time their belonging to and interaction with their own communities had been cut off. According to records, very few returned to their places of origin to illuminate their people with the 'civilising' light of the National Torch. Most refused to return to their communities to 'redeem their brothers and sisters'. They were exiled into an identity limbo where their mother tongue was denied but neither were they recognised as perfect speakers of the national language. The Casa del Estudiante Indígena insisted that pupils should not forget their languages because it was through them that they would be able to civilise their brothers and sisters – to transmit nationalist ideas about progress. One of the few good decisions the Casa took was to create language clubs so the pupils could teach each other their mother tongues, but at the end of the day Indigenous languages were considered a temporary means until Spanish could replace them.

If we examine these 'experiments' closely, what's surprising is not that cultural and linguistic diversity are disappearing, but rather that it still exists at all. In the movement to recognise Indigenous rights, we're proud of the ways we resist but still wish we didn't have to. Resistance implies the existence of an aggression. Resistance is exhausting. While we are proud of our five hundred years of resistance, ideally we'd live in a country where there was no need for us to resist, and that country is the one we are interested in building: a country where we wouldn't need to resist in order to speak our languages, or just to be ourselves.

17 April, 2013

# A SOLDIER IN EVERY SON?

*Until lions have their own historians, the history of the hunt will always glorify the hunter.*

AFRICAN PROVERB

It strikes me as a curious phenomenon, to say the least, that among the action taken to recognise original languages, the translation of the Mexican national anthem has become a main point of contention. On 8 December, 2005, Article 39 of the Law of National Symbols was reformed to make it possible to translate the anthem into the other languages spoken in this country. This had not previously been permitted and, as far as I'm concerned, that speaks volumes. Since then, the National Institute of Indigenous Languages has established a programme to translate the national anthem. However,

*Imagine that an Ayuujk athlete wins a gold medal, and while being interviewed by the press they pull out and wave the Mixe flag instead of the Mexican one? Hahahahaha… I can just imagine the comments and reactions.*

*(And when asked whether they feel Mexican, they reply: 'I'm Mixe, I only have a Mexican passport as the result of a historical misfortune that I'll happily tell you more about' [Paraphrasing, once again, the Mapuche journalist Pedro Cayuqueo]). Tee hee hee.*

❶                        *20 Aug, 2016*

the anthem, which glorifies war above all else, has for many years been translated by other educational institutions and organisations, and through personal initiatives (there's even a version in Plautdietsch, the Mennonite language).

But what is the goal of translating the national anthem? One of independent Mexico's main concerns was the creation of symbols that would encourage the idea of national unity. After all, what did a mestizo living in San Cristóbal de las Casas have in common with an Indigenous Kumeyaay from Baja California? Not language, not food, not history; and yet they belonged to a single country for reasons completely out of their hands and had to be made to feel part of that country. So many different peoples with their own histories and languages, with entirely distinct identities, had to be grouped together under a single nation state. A country which, when it came to settling on its political division into independent, sovereign state entities, failed to take into account the territorial and cultural differences of the peoples that comprised it. As a consequence, the integration of Indigenous peoples into the new homeland left much to be desired; testimonies on the wars of independence, foreign invasions and the Mexican Revolution confirm that Indigenous people were accused of being bad patriots, of not adequately internalising the nationalist discourse, of being bad Mexicans, of not loving Mexico, of not being the 'soldiers in every son' that the anthem claims were sent to the homeland from up above. Save for a few exceptions, conscription was the main reason Indigenous people were incorporated into battles to save the homeland, not a sudden rush of love for Mexico, which, as a state, wanted nothing more than to nullify their cultural realities.

So what is the goal of translating the national anthem into Mexico's original and minoritised languages? Will Indigenous peoples' sense of belonging to this nation state increase

*When a revolutionary tells me the main goal is to save the homeland or the nation… I immediately switch off.*

X                     *5 Mar, 2014*

with every translation? Will these languages become more highly valued? I doubt it very much. The lyrics of the national anthem, as well as being closely linked to their historical context, do not reflect the country's cultural diversity, not to mention that even for most native speakers of Spanish they are barely comprehensible ('masiosare' instead of 'mas si osare un extraño enemigo…' – *but if some enemy outlander should dare…*). I think there's little sense in wasting so many resources on these translations. In any case, if the goal is to achieve greater inclusion and esteem for language diversity, we would have to compose a new anthem or follow South Africa's example: at the launch of the 2010 Football World Cup, their national anthem, learned this way by all South Africans, was sung in Afrikaans, Xhosa, Sotho, Zulu and English, one verse in each language.

Can you imagine the impact it would have if all Mexicans (regardless of their first language) were to sing a national anthem with verses in Plautdietsch, Spanish, Maya and Nahuatl? Now that would truly deserve to be called a 'national' anthem.

Then again, nationalists have always struck me as verging on dangerous.

*My Mixe ancestors who so resisted paying taxes to the Aztecs must want to die all over again whenever they see us paying homage to that crest of the eagle devouring the serpent…*

f                     *12 Oct, 2015*

25 July, 2012

# CUT OUT THEIR TONGUES

The ubiquitous positive depiction of multiculturalism, plurilingualism and diversity itself cannot be explained without specific social and historical context.[12] Previously, ideas about welfare and progress were closely linked, at least in Mexico, to the elimination of differences, one of the most visible of which is the number of languages spoken in this country. With a view to a social and linguistic standardisation that would create Mexican citizens all under equal circumstances, Hispanicisation programmes were implemented that continue to have repercussions today. The worst thing about this process was not that the Indigenous population learned Spanish (an entirely valid goal – learning another language is both desirable and highly enjoyable); it was that everything possible was done to make sure that those people stopped speaking their own languages. That, and the mechanisms used to achieve this. It might sound contradictory, but the main goal of Hispanicisation was not Hispanicisation as such, but rather to combat the use

> *The Indigenous 'question' doesn't just affect Indigenous people.*
>
> 𝕏                    *15 Feb, 2012*

---

[12]   See Flores Magón, R., *Antología* (Mexico City: UNAM, 1993).

'As I understand it, "Indigenous" is a category that does not allow for a different future, but rather implies maintaining the status quo when it comes to today's struggles and dependencies. "Mixe" and "Mesoamerican" do allow us to glimpse a different future and indeed a different present, in which identity is not constructed exclusively in relation to the nation state. Besides, "Indigenous" only covers 494 of the 9000 years of Mixe or Mesoamerican history (if we take the domestication of corn as its genesis) or 3200 years (if we take the Olmec culture as its beginning). Surely the use of the term "Indigenous" by the nation state is an ontological contradiction? Seeing as it's a tacit recognition of the failure of the national project' / Sebastián van Doesburg.

16 Dec, 2015

of original languages.

I'm shocked by the gallery of bodily and psychological punishments inflicted in this context to eliminate the use of Indigenous languages, especially because, beyond struggling against a language's very existence, it involved regulating the strictly personal sphere of specific individuals. I can only imagine the psychological repercussions of those punishments – the consequences for people's daily lives and their own sense of self-worth.

An Ayuujk woman told me that when she migrated to the city she was beaten for speaking her mother tongue, and so understood that it would be best to forget it; but when she returned to her community, she was beaten again for refusing to speak Ayuujk. When she went back to school she had to endure further blows until she could speak exclusively in Spanish. 'What's the right thing to do this time?' she asked me, 'speak Mixe or not speak Mixe? I'd like to know what the next excuse for a beating will be.' A primary school teacher told me a similar story. He attended a rural teachers' college where he became convinced that teaching exclusively Spanish and

126

suppressing Mixe was the best way of bringing progress to his village, and so he poured his heart and soul into this method for decades. Now his children complain that he never taught them to speak Ayuujk and new teachers use him as an example of bad linguistic practice in the classroom. 'What is correct these days?' 'What is the right discourse?' he wondered, and I wonder now too.

All that torture, carried out in the name of eliminating Indigenous languages, bore fruit; the message that Indigenous languages are just useless 'dialects' impeding progress was internalised so thoroughly by both Indigenous and non-Indigenous people that it was no longer even necessary to beat people to convince them to stop speaking them. The discourse is now changing, and the days when you would receive a lash for every word in Tzotzil or a fine for every word in Mixe might seem distant, but there's no question that punishments still exist: some years ago I read a news article describing the case of a girl who was tied up for hours for speaking Nahuatl in the classroom, and the case of a defendant forced to speak only Spanish. Not long ago I was forbidden to act as interpreter for a patient in hospital.

Speaking a mother tongue that isn't Spanish has remained closely linked to rapped knuckles, the humiliation of public mockery, the sting of pinched flesh, the despair that follows every punishment. There are so many violent ways of exercising power over the other and it's a terrible shame that forcing someone to stop speaking their mother tongue forms part of that inventory of torture. Who can be held accountable?

Beyond the discourse, both new and historical, there is no denying that original languages are

*When the government says, 'Speak your language so it doesn't die', it's like being told to 'breathe deeply' while you're being strangled…*

X                    *5 Feb, 2015*

127

being eliminated as the direct consequence of centuries of systematic violation of Indigenous people's human rights. For this reason, I'd go so far as to say that the death of a language, more than a linguistic issue, is a human rights issue, and it is on that basis that it should be explained.

7 June, 2012

# IS IT WORTH PROMOTING THE USE OF INDIGENOUS LANGUAGES?

In my community, Ayutla, the Mixe language is under threat, as it is in many communities. Compared to my own childhood, there are now fewer and fewer spaces where Mixe is used and transmission from one generation to another is not guaranteed. Although the censuses indicate that more than 80% of the community population can speak Mixe, this doesn't necessarily mean that it's spoken daily in all areas of the community.

Like all Mixe speakers, I confess I have huge affection (irrational like all true loves) for the specific way Mixe is spoken in my community: I like how we

*The fact that I speak Mixe today is thanks to thousands, yes, thousands of years of everyone passing down their language to the next generation until it reached my lips. Can it be that my generation will be responsible for interrupting that flow, and that when we die our language will be buried with us because we failed in the task of passing it on to the next generation?*

                    *15 Feb, 2016*

*Kutyu'umëp is a Mixe verb that specifically describes the act of the moon becoming full. I only hear older people use it these days, but I try to use it myself on nights like this when the moon is bright, sketching the silhouette of the Tukyo'm mountains. Po' means moon, and today: kutyu'umëp ja po'.*

                    *22 Feb, 2016*

129

conjugate verbs, our obscure etymologies, the way we ask questions and our unique intonation when speaking. As well as for obvious reasons, it makes me incredibly sad to think that Ayutla Mixe might disappear one day, because the Mixe of my community is unique and irreplaceable and because it marks us out among the different Mixe peoples.

Some years ago, I began in a rather naïve way to carry out activities promoting the use of Mixe in my community. Together with several others, I started Mixe language get-togethers, public speaking contests, vocabulary competitions for children, a syllable nucleus bingo, a numbers bingo, concerts in Mixe and, more recently, publications. I spoke to anyone who would listen about the importance of preserving our language, of passing it on to children, of using it every day, of giving it new spaces where it could be used.

> *Being conscious of the importance of speaking your language is NOT enough to ensure it's passed on to the next generation.*
>
> X                   *12 June, 2013*

Even though these activities have, to some degree, led to greater recognition of the seriousness of the situation, I have to accept they've contributed very little, if anything, to increasing the use of Mixe in a concrete way. Disillusioned, I realised that many people only spoke Mixe to their children if I was nearby (out of courtesy, because of my interest), or that, even though they used it in conversation with me, this didn't mean they'd now use it with people they'd previously have spoken to in Spanish. Generally speaking, even the people to whom I 'preached' most often about the importance of preserving the use of Ayuujk did not change their linguistic habits.

After the initial shock, I asked myself seriously what right I had to try to influence other people's linguistic habits. Why was I trying to change the behaviour of people who were 'choosing' to speak Spanish to their children instead of Mixe? Then again, I'd always been convinced of the importance of passing on and strengthening Mixe. What was the best way to promote and strengthen it?

> *If what you're doing (however you're promoting the preservation of linguistic diversity) doesn't result, directly or indirectly, in a child learning the same mother tongue as their parents where otherwise they would not have… then you need to reconsider your way of working…*
>
> ❍         *18 Oct, 2012*

Who was this important to? Something wasn't right.

I realised that the use of Mixe cannot be promoted with words, perhaps not even with arguments, but rather through concrete, enjoyable experiences. Living in that language should not be promoted as a duty but rather as a rich, joyful possibility. People who have stopped passing on and using Mixe can, after a while, become quite convinced of its importance and yet still not be able to change their everyday linguistic habit of speaking in Spanish to their young children. Linguistic ideologisation doesn't necessarily result in a change in linguistic habits. This is clear from the many people involved in the struggle for recognition of community rights, or from bilingual education activists who, despite knowing the importance of Mixe better than anyone, have not passed the language on to their own children. Like any habit, linguistic ones are hard to break, and can resist even the best arguments.

That said, I became even more convinced that no one decides to stop speaking a language unless its speakers have been exposed to constant and systematic discrimination. It would be strange, at the very least, for a couple in Berlin whose mother tongue is German to decide not to teach that language to their children and instead teach them only English. The couple might try and get their children to learn English, too, but this will never mean they don't want them to inherit their mother tongue, German. The apparent 'decision' to stop speaking a language such as Mixe is struggling under centuries of discrimination and full-on opposition to its use.

We can't just preach the importance of Mixe to speakers who are abandoning it; we also have to combat all the social and political factors that make it a discriminated language. So in truth, I don't want to promote the passing down of Mixe from one generation to another; I want to do away with the political and social factors that stop what should be natural: learning the language spoken by your parents, your aunts and uncles, your grandparents and your community. If speakers of the Mixe language weren't discriminated against and their linguistic rights weren't violated, if we received education in our languages and were taught to read and write in them, if the health and justice systems took Mixe seriously and provided trained interpreters, if we had publications, grammars and learning materials in Mixe, if all this were a reality and yet someone still decided to stop teaching Mixe to their children, then I would think it strange but I would neither criticise their decision nor try to change it.

*The greater the autonomy of Indigenous peoples, the more likely their language is to be strengthened. I refer you to the evidence. I no longer understand linguistic revitalisation as separate from the struggle for Indigenous peoples' autonomy. Everything else is just folklore.*

**f** 9 Feb, 2016

But until that's the case, it's not enough for me to insist on the importance of Mixe to its speakers; I also have to demand that the Mexican state ensure fair conditions for them and their language. I cannot do the first without demanding the second.

I understand, on the other hand, that at the end of the day the life of the Mixe language is in the hands of the speakers themselves. Faced with this reality, neither sermons nor ideology – much less reprimands – seem to be a good response. The response in cases such as that of my own community is, I believe, to promote enjoyment – to give chess lessons, a photography workshop or a karate class entirely in Mixe would be more effective at preserving the language than a Mixe language course. That's what I believe. For now.

So, is it worth promoting Indigenous languages? Yes, but, as ever, the question is *how*. How do we go about it?

13 Aug, 2014

*When someone says to me: 'the conditions don't exist to do what you want', I always respond: 'well let's step back a bit and work to create the conditions for what we want to achieve'.*

27 Sept, 2017

Ⓕ 23 Mar, 2017

# Romantic love is to the patriarchy what nationalism is to the state.

---

𝕏 1 Aug, 2018

How many of you would speak an Indigenous language if racism and the state project had not meant that your grandparents or parents had decided that 'for your own good' they'd better not pass on their language to you? To be mestizo is to be de-indigenised by the state.

𝕏 9 June, 2018

– So how do you feel after five hundred years of resistance?
– Exhausted.

---

Ⓕ 1 Sept, 2011

## Feeling is tiring.

---

𝕏 10 July, 2016

Erratum II: For *Anthology of Mexican Poetry* read *Anthology of Mexican Poetry by Spanish Speakers*

---

Ⓕ 21 Oct, 2015

# You're so state, I'm all nation...

## 2 Aug, 2017

I find it funny that the Mexican Constitution (and those of several other countries in these parts) says in one of its very first articles: 'The Mexican nation is one and indivisible'. I mean, if states really were one and indivisible there would be no need to say so. 'One doesn't ask about what's plain to see', said Juan Gabriel, aka Juanga, except I guess in this case it's more like 'one doesn't decree what is true'.

---

## 17 April, 2016

You, me, the Commissary for Communal Property measuring our land and then handing over our proof of ownership, I don't know, think about it… #HighlandLove

## 11 Dec, 2018

**You're not going to believe this, but I just had the following conversation with my gran:**

**Gran:**
…Then write me a prayer of petition for mass tomorrow, for the anniversary of my brother Aurelio's death.

**Me:**
On the computer, right?

**Gran:**
Yes, and uh, don't forget to add a request for John Lennon's eternal rest.

**Me:**
John Lennon?!?

**Gran:**
Yes, the other day I saw a film about his death, he died in December, a violent death, and I don't want his soul hanging around in this world. This way he won't come back on Day of the Dead.

---

## 13 Aug, 2015

Nationalism's success lies in its ability to convert ideology into feelings.

# PART III:

# WHAT SHALL WE CALL HER,
MATARILERILERÓ?

# DOES LINGUISTIC ACTIVISM
# EXIST IN MEXICO?

*Activism in defence of animal rights is better articulated
than activism in defence of linguistic diversity,
as well as more common.*

## CONVERSATIONS OVER COFFEE

Last month in Oaxaca, Dr Lylle
Campbell gave a talk on the Catalogue
of Endangered Languages, available to
access via the Endangered Languages
Project website.[13] As you might expect,
the predictions are no cause for
optimism. Every three months a language dies somewhere
in the world; 6% of world languages have fewer than
ten speakers; and 227 languages have died since 1960.
For this researcher from the University of Hawaii and
the team in charge of putting together the Catalogue of
Endangered Languages, the accelerated, unprecedented
loss of world languages today constitutes one of humanity's main priorities. Language loss is a direct reflection of

---

[13] The aim of the Endangered Languages Project, as its website
indicates, is to be 'an online resource for samples and research on
endangered languages as well as a forum for advice and best practices
for those working to strengthen linguistic diversity'.

the fact that the linguistic rights of millions of people are not being respected. Mexico, obviously, is no exception.

Language activists in different parts of the world have made great strides in tackling this situation: Hawaiian, a language that was previously at high risk of disappearing, is now more robust. It's possible to go all the way through from preschool to university studying in Hawaiian, and its number of speakers has increased spectacularly. Similarly, in New Zealand, Māori language nests have created new speakers, and there are various other comparable examples around the world. If new generations are to learn at-risk languages, extensive activist efforts and active militancy in support of the cause are among the steps that must be taken.

In Mexico there are many movements to strengthen Indigenous languages, which have fewer and fewer speakers; however, these efforts concentrate mainly on developing writing skills and very little on ensuring that children learn to speak Mixe, Huichol or Otomi as their mother tongue. Despite extraordinary efforts, often executed against all odds, these initiatives are unfortunately very fragmented. It is not enough to translate the national anthem into Nahuatl, to record songs and organise vocab bingo nights (*mea culpa*); we have to make sure all these actions are part of a strategic plan that aims to increase the number of children speaking languages such as Nahuatl, Otomi and Mixe. Measures need to be taken on several fronts in a systematic, planned way, in order to have the greatest possible impact.

I understand that activism always comes from civil society pressuring states and governments to take measures to achieve a goal and to propose concrete action and programmes. To give just one example, Indigenous women's activism in defence of gender equality has managed to get the issue onto the agenda of national, international and governmental organisations. Indigenous feminists have spaces for education, are trained in advocacy and carry out strategic planning to achieve their goals; there are funds and NGOs specialised in Indigenous gender equality and awards recognising their work. The Indigenous women's movement undoubtedly still faces many challenges, but compared to linguistic activism, they are miles ahead.

Although many of us are conscious of the gravity of the loss of linguistic diversity in Mexico, the truth is that we've failed to come together as a unified movement. There are no spaces dedicated to training us about the issue, no NGOs specialised in linguistic revitalisation, no strategic plan to reverse the loss in the short, medium or long term, no planned advocacy to force the state to take effective measures, no strategy of concrete actions to be carried out. I'd go as far as to say there is no single linguistic activism movement in Mexico.

By saying this, I don't mean to dismiss the extraordinary efforts of many people and organisations fighting daily to improve the situation on various fronts, but I think we need to come together more; think how great it would be if the activists working with Mozilla Mexico to localise (translate) the Firefox browser into Southern Zapotec, Chatino or Mixe were to collaborate with lawyers from the Centro Profesional Indígena de Asesoría, Defensa y Traducción A. C. (Professional Indigenous Centre for Advice, Legal Defence and Translation) who work to protect the linguistic rights of Indigenous language speakers incarcerated without access to an interpreter during their trial. I'm imagining writers in Indigenous languages talking to people who assess language vitality and then collaborating with political scientists who could help us influence the public and political agenda, as Tajëëw Díaz explained to me so well. I imagine, too, that it would be possible to better link up the academic work of linguists with the everyday work of activism.

 There's much to be done, and the work seems as immense as the challenge; but we have to get started. Fortunately, social interactions are mediated through languages, so it's possible to work towards linguistic strengthening in various spaces and thus secure new generations of speakers. I have the impression that in several areas, including in the Indigenous movement itself, language continues to be understood as closely related to cultural manifestations such as dance, song and the traditional practices grouped under the vague term 'cultural activities'. I believe it's more than this; the struggle to slow the loss of linguistic diversity is above all a political issue that's intimately connected to the struggle for the autonomy of Indigenous peoples in Mexico. For as long as we fail to recognise this, the 'rescuing of languages' will be seen in the same way as the 'rescuing of traditional dress', as someone once explained to me.

> *Indigenous people don't get involved in politics? PURLEASE, the very category 'Indigenous' IS a political category (not a racial or a cultural category, but racialised and culturalised, that's for sure). (I said in politics, NOT party politics – two very different things).*
>
>  *15 Oct, 2016*

In addition, we need to build alliances with other movements and with native speakers of Spanish. I believe we could achieve a great deal if the topic of language loss were also part of the Indigenous movement's fight for autonomy, of the defence of territory and the rights of Indigenous women. We need to position the topic in various spaces where a fight for the recognition of Indigenous peoples' rights and human rights in general is taking place. Language extinction is one of the direct consequences of social injustice, and it should be addressed within that context.

It's a bit disheartening when those directly involved with issues relating to Indigenous peoples remark that all we need to do to 'rescue' a language is set up competitions for 'their poems' or performances of 'their traditional songs', as I once heard someone condescendingly say. No, it involves something more radical. Language is not just a 'cultural issue', understood as a spectacle; it's not folklore: the Indigenous movement should understand itself in this country's different languages, should debate its own identity and aims in this country's languages. The Indigenous movement should make Indigenous languages official and use them for analysis and to put together proposals. As the cases of Basque and Catalan have shown, the language issue is clearly a political issue, too. Until we can make this happen, we'll likely end up taking a lot of action that will only rarely succeed in slowing the loss of speakers and spaces where Mexican languages are used.

*It's the Ministry of Finance, the Treasury, the Supreme Audit Office, and all those who try to collect property tax on communal lands who are in DESPERATE need of courses, intensive workshops and conferences, who should be obliged to learn about Indigenous peoples' right to autonomy, free determination and consultation, about ILO Convention 169 and all the rest of it... culture? what about it?*

*12 Feb, 2016*

Activists fighting for Indigenous peoples' rights in Mexico could also become activists fighting for Mexico's languages. If they don't, the trend will continue: the children of leaders of the Indigenous movement and bilingual teachers will remain much less likely to acquire their parents' language instead of Spanish as a mother tongue.

This situation poses questions to which we must respond as a group, because I don't yet have clear answers: How do we build linguistic activism? How do we put together concrete, gradual strategies? How do we advocate for specific policies and programmes to be implemented in addition to the many initiatives that already exist? Where do we receive training to carry out this work? How do we slow down the death of languages and the violation of their speakers' linguistic rights?

22 May, 2014

# WHAT SHALL WE CALL HER, MATARILERILERÓ?

*I wanted to be called Batman!! And also to be Swiss, so I could eat chocolate all day long!!*

(Miguelito)
Children's rights, as described by Mafalda

Tii mxëë? This is how we ask someone's name in Ayutla Mixe. However, because of the polysemy of the word xëë, which also means 'day', the question can also be translated as 'what is your day?' which reminds us that in the Mesoamerican tradition a person was given a name according to the date on which they were born. The name of the famous Mixtec king from the codices, Ocho Venado-Garra de Jaguar (Eight Deer-Jaguar Claw) indicated the date on which he was born according to the Mixtec calendar. The name-dates of other characters can also be found in the codices that narrate his deeds: his father was called Cinco Lagarto-Sol de Lluvia (Five Lizard-Rain Sun), his mother was Nueve Águila-Flor del Cacao (Nine Eagle-Cacao Flower) and one of his sisters was called Seis Lagartija-Abanico de Jade (Six Gecko-Jade Fan).

I suppose that during the colonial era, this tradition of giving people calendar names was displaced by the

Catholic calendar of saints' days, which also gave people names according to their date of birth – hence the fact that a person's saint's day was the same as their birthday. Until recently in my community, many families gave new-born children a saint's name according to the day they were born, and, just as in the pre-Hispanic era, this was not a matter of choice. The names of saints were adapted to the phonological patterns of Mixe: José became Xaap, María became Maniiy, Juan became Xëwään and Elena became Len, to cite just a few examples.

*Looking for a name for a baby? What about Yoots… It means 'cloud' in Ayutla Mixe and in other varieties too. So their soul may always be as light as the clouds atop our mountains.*

 *9 July, 2017*

These days there are no limitations on parents when it comes to choosing names for their children, or at least in theory. Some civil registry offices explicitly prohibit names that clearly lend themselves to euphemism or jokes when combined with the parents' surnames: Elba Zurita ('el basurita' – piece of crap), Rosamiel Fierro ('rózame el fierro' – rub my dick) or Alan Brito Delgado ('alambrito delgado' – skinny dick).

Given the country's linguistic diversity, Indigenous peoples' language rights should guarantee that names in Mexican languages other than Spanish will not be discriminated against in the civil registry office. However, this is far from being a reality. While names in English are increasingly common and the civil registry increasingly respects the original language spelling of names such as Jessica, attempts to register a child with a name in Mixe, Otomi or Tepehua are often still problematic, and this constitutes a clear violation of linguistic rights.

A few years ago, one of my uncles wanted to give his first son a Mixe name. When he went to the civil registry office, the official on duty used every means possible to dissuade him. He argued that the child would struggle when learning to write their name and that other children would make fun of him at school, until eventually, the boy's father

> *Looking for a baby name? How about Mejy, which means 'sea' but is also used to describe any large body of water, such as a lake or lagoon. It's an Ayuujk word, Tukyo'm Ayuujk.*
>
> **0**                    *27 Aug, 2017*

still unconvinced, he simply said it was not possible and that he should choose a name in Spanish. Only after much effort and trouble was my uncle able to register his son with the name he wanted.

This is a common story. In the case of an Otomi couple who wanted to name their daughter in that language, the parents faced a huge number of diffi-culties and discriminatory comments before they were allowed to register the Otomi name, which

> *Looking for a baby name? Anaa.*
> *It's the Ayutla Mixe word for the thunder that accompanies lightning. With a double a: Anaa. Powerful, no?*
>
> **0**                    *17 May, 2017*

includes a dieresis and a vowel marked with an accent. One of the most frequent excuses is that the computers used to register the names do not accept symbols or letters that do not belong to Spanish; my friend Tajëëw (the name of a Mixe divinity) told me that at one stage she had to give up on using her diereses on official documents because, unlike typewriters, the registry system on the computers couldn't adequately input her name. Rather than putting a sensitivity course in place for public servants working in civil registries and adapting the computer system to the context of linguistic diversity, the official response has been to try to convince parents not to choose

147

*In Ayutla Mixe, 'surname' is 'xëënëkon'.*

*I know that other Mixe varieties use a borrowing from Spanish. I propose that, if we're going to use borrowings, we borrow them from other varieties of Mixe.*

**☉**                    *9 Sept, 2017*

names in original Mexican languages.

A few months ago, I read in the news that an Indigenous couple had to demonstrate that they belong to an original people before they were allowed to give their son an Indigenous name. That's like saying that non-Indigenous people can't be called Xóchitl or Cuauhtémoc and, even more absurd, that you have to belong to a certain nation to have a certain name: according to this logic, only Jewish people can be called Myriam or Abraham and only US Americans can be called Jennifer or Elizabeth.

The fact that parents are choosing more and more often to give their children names in Indigenous languages has strong activist potential. It's also true that the names themselves reflect many aspects of Indigenous culture and history. My friend Ana told me that in Holland people used not to have surnames, and it was only during Napoleon's invasion that the population was obliged to choose them. By way of protest, many chose surnames that were mocking or scatological, which have continued to be passed down and preserved to this day.

The civil registry office's refusal to register names in Indigenous languages speaks volumes about the kind of relationships the Mexican state establishes with Indigenous communities. The civil registry has been necessary for the state but not really for communities themselves. For linguistic rights to genuinely be respected, the government needs to implement convincing measures to ensure that any Mexican, whether Indigenous or not, can assign a name to their child in any of Mexico's languages.

The tension between states and Indigenous peoples regarding the obligation to use the civil registry, and the prejudices and discrimination involved in this process, are on display in Priscila Padilla's documentary *Nacidos el 31 de diciembre* (Born on 31 December): when registering more than ten thousand Indigenous Wayuu people in Colombia, public servants working at the civil register took advantage of the fact that most Wayuu do not speak Spanish to change their Indigenous names to similar-sounding, derisive nicknames on each of their identity cards. They were assigned names such as Alka Seltzer, Coito (coitus), Zapato (shoe), Marihuana, Paraguas (umbrella), Cosita Rica (tasty little thing) and Raspahierro (dick rub). What's more, all were registered as having been born on 31 December – absolutely all of them. Some time later, the Wayuu began the process of seeking compensation from the Colombian state for the damage caused (see the YouTube video 'Nacimos el 31 de diciembre').

These situations reveal that the government needs to try harder to make sure the right to choose a name in an Indigenous language is upheld. The problem is not that some people do not speak Spanish; the main problem is that civil registry offices have become one of the great bastions  of linguistic and cultural prejudice, where functionaries often show very little awareness of the multicultural environment in which they carry out their work. Let's hope that, soon, being called John, Pëjy or Rodrigo will be equally valid and, above all, equally possible; that this can become a country where it's less complicated to call your child Jaxyëë than – as one set of parents allegedly wanted – Hitler.

3 July, 2013

# NEWSPAPERS AND MAGAZINES IN INDIGENOUS LANGUAGES?

## THE PRESS AND INDIGENOUS COMMUNICATION

Happily, there is an increasing number of Indigenous communities creating their own media. In a country where licences are state property, I think it's crucial for Indigenous communities and peoples to develop their own media without being penalised. Considering the history of the formation of the Mexican state, one would hope Indigenous peoples could at least make use of their right to autonomy and free self-determination by using media such as the radio and television without having to be criminalised, harassed or accused of being illegal, as has been the case throughout their history. Despite everything, community radio stations are on the rise and there are also experiments with television in Indigenous territories, as well as an increasingly rich audio-visual scene. These community activities are closely linked to the strengthening of languages, to reflections on culture, and to political and identity processes in relation to the state.

Among these experiences of communication in Indigenous communities, written communication has specific characteristics. While community radio and audio-visual production seem to be on the up, written communication is advancing less quickly. The oral nature of radio, television and audio-visual media in general seems to facilitate the process. Anyone with a radio or TV can be part of an audience that enjoys community media programming. In my town, my grandmother used to tune into the local Konk Anaa Community Radio or neighbouring town Tlahuitoltepec's Jënpoj Community Radio while she heated up the comal; over the course of the day, she could listen to the news, a programme about music, a debate forum about transgenic corn or the final of a regional football tournament in Mixe.

In contrast, there's a more complicated process of audience creation involved in developing written forms of communication. It's true that there already exists a written press in national languages other than Spanish, and that more publications are emerging, but there is no comparison with community radio and other media that don't depend entirely on writing in terms of the enthusiasm and frequency with which they're emerging.

> *The foundation of writing is 'visual' symbols; the foundation of the oral tradition is not the voice but rather memory.*
>
> 𝕏                    *1 Sept, 2014*

I personally know of few examples of written press or periodicals in Indigenous languages. In the Mixe region I know there was the *Revista Uxpijy* in Tlahuitoltepec, which published bilingually and 'whose objective was to register community memory, which strengthens not only the Ayuujk community's language, historical memory and Indigenous sense of identity, but also opens spaces of participation, especially for women.'

*K'a'ajsaj* is a bilingual newspaper in the Maya language published by the Universidad de Oriente in Yucatán, whose main purpose is to 'disseminate Maya culture in all its forms'.

In the article 'La literatura de los Binnizá: Zapotecos del Istmo' (The Literature of the Binnizá: The Isthmus Zapotecs'[14] the Juchitecan poet Irma Pineda discusses *Revista Neza* (whose title means 'the path, the right way' in Zapotec), which was published in Mexico City by the Sociedad Nueva de Estudiantes Juchitecos (New Society of Juchitecan Students).

While it lasted, the *Revista Iguanazul*, founded by Judith Santopietro, promoted literature, art and the oral traditions of Mexico's original peoples. As well as publishing periodicals, Iguanazul also published cartonera books, mostly in Nahuatl.

In addition to those mentioned here, other short-lived periodicals are emerging increasingly often, and there are undoubtedly many more initiatives I'm unaware of emerging within Indigenous communities. However, almost all of them are bilingual publications; while most Spanish language publications are monolingual, the Indigenous language press still seems to need facing-page Spanish. To me, this situation is evidence that the appropriation of the written press as a means of communication requires an extraordinary effort: to create readers in Indigenous languages. Despite this titanic task, I believe it's crucial we start this work and try to appropriate this means of communication within Indigenous communities. At the same time

---

[14] Pineda, I. 'La literatura de los Binnizá: Zapotecas del Istmo', *De la oralidad a la palabra escrita: Estudio sobre el rescate de las voces originarias en el sur de México* (Mexico: El Colegio de Guerrero and Editora Laguna, 2012), 293–310.

as demanding and appropriating radio, television and other audiovisual media, we must demand and appropriate printing presses, found publishing houses and support periodical publications, all the while building a reading public. The movement to promote Indigenous communication cannot leave behind the written press in Indigenous languages. It should be defended as one of the movement's demands and as one of the fundamental pillars of action.

Fortunately, the internet is sketching out a way forward: there are ever more pages that use writing in Indigenous languages as a communication tool – but that will be the topic of another piece.

*We could have our own community servers: communal ownership of the land, communal ownership of the internet #MXlanguageactivism*

X    *3 Oct, 2014*

4 Sept, 2013

# MULTILINGUAL FIREFOX

'I searched for content in the language I speak, and cyberspace yielded nothing', says Rodrigo Pérez, a Zapotec speaker from San Andrés Paxtlán in the Sierra Sur of Oaxaca and one of the key figures overseeing the localisation (translation) of Firefox, Mozilla's famous browser, into various Mexican languages. Just as in the non-virtual world, the imbalance between the world's many languages is reflected in cyberspace: speakers of Indigenous languages can rarely use them to access virtual content or spaces.

The project seeking to localise Firefox into Indigenous languages began in 2008 when the Mozilla Mexico community, the organisation known as Indígenas Sin Fronteras (Indigenous Peoples Without Borders), and the Linux group at the Universidad Regiomontana formed the first working group for the localisation of Zapotec, a language belonging to one of Mexico's largest language families, the Oto-Manguean family. Teams working on Maya, Nahuatl, and Tzotzil were later incorporated, and there are now thirty-six pilot projects in other Indigenous languages, twelve of them Mexican. The languages in which the work is most advanced are Sierra Sur Zapotec, Nahuatl and Maya; it is hoped that this year (2011) they will reach the goal of 70% translated material and so become the first official Mexican Indigenous languages of Firefox.

The localisers are Indigenous language speakers who form part of a virtual community known as Mozilla Nativo. Each collaborative localisation project is begun by a speaker wishing to carry out the localisation; that person becomes the project administrator. All they have to do is register themselves on the Mozilla page and, after receiving some general guidelines, begin to translate collaboratively with the help of the online tool Pootle.

 The administrator and general coordinator for each language has all the permissions from the online tool to carry out the translations. If someone else is interested, they can join the work using the same platform. They register themselves on the system and then are given orientation on the state of the project and its tools. The project administrator checks the linked translations done by the rest of the team and endorses the final versions. In this way, an online community is formed, one that can interact, discuss terms to be used, the nuances of texts, and the progress of the localisation work, despite not knowing one another in person. Any new participant is welcome to join the project, with each individual deciding how many hours they wish to dedicate to the localisation efforts. The more active participants there are, the quicker the project advances.

Those who collaborate on these localisation projects in Indigenous languages are volunteers. They do the work for free and there is no single person responsible for each topic or activity; rather, teams of workers are created in which the coordinators are those who have most experience. This working dynamic means that teams are comprised of people with a huge range of backgrounds, ages and levels of education. There are no hierarchies within the teams, and the work is carried out horizontally, so that everyone can contribute to achieving the necessary 70% to make a given language official.

In the words of Rodrigo Pérez, it's important to use free software when promoting the presence of Mexican languages in cyberspace, because, unlike with private software, free software allows for modifications to be made. The work is done in a collaborative way that promotes fair, democratic access to new information technologies. In this sense, there are similarities between the social organisation of many Indigenous communities in Oaxaca and the virtual communities on free software such as Mozilla or Wikipedia: in both types of community, collaboration and group work are fundamental for their development; each person's work contributes to achieving the general objectives. In other words, Indigenous communities and free software have in common that they are based on communality and mutual aid.

The Mozilla Nativo community faces no small challenge: to become an official language of the desktop version of Firefox, 41,000 words must be translated. This involves an average of three hours of work every day for approximately six months. Translators also face additional challenges: they have to fully understand the meaning and purpose of the content, create neologisms wherever necessary and master writing in languages whose orthographies are often not entirely fixed. The localisers act as translators not only between cultures but also between spaces: the virtual world and that of the language in question, with all its peculiarities. Isaura de los Santos, a speaker of Chatino, a language in the Oto-Manguean family that has a fairly complex tonal system, is in charge of localising her language on Firefox. She explains that, for her, the work she's been doing for some time now, alongside a network of people, has been fundamental to the teaching of literacy in Chatino. Translating Firefox into Indigenous languages necessarily implies, in one way or other, creating a network of collaborators.

For this reason, it's important for translators to work closely with their communities, and with people involved in the process of strengthening their languages and developing their writing systems. In order to achieve this, Mozilla also promotes 'translatathons', intensive days of translation in which an entire community can participate in localising their language on Firefox and so make huge advances in just a few days. 'Translatathons' allow the elderly, young people, women, children, and anyone else interested to participate, collaborate, and discuss the linked translations and the neologisms being created for use on Firefox.

As well as the desktop version of Firefox, Mozilla has developed Firefox Android for tablets and Firefox OS for mobile, both of which are also in the process of being translated. Given the famous digital divide, the Indigenous language version of Firefox for mobile phones is an excellent option because it allows for ties to be established with initiatives such as community-owned mobile phone services in areas where internet access is still not guaranteed.

In the face of catastrophic forecasts for linguistic diversity (UNESCO calculates that in the next hundred years more than half of the world's languages will have disappeared), working towards languages' presence in the virtual world is a way of working to avoid, insofar as is possible, the disappearance of languages that are continually subject to discrimination.

Many participants in localisation efforts, including Rodrigo Pérez (Zapotec), Isaura de los Santos (San

Miguel Panixtlahuaca Chatino) and Netzahualcóyotl López (Santa María Yucuiti Mixtec), are convinced that speakers of all Mexico's languages have the right, just like speakers of languages in other parts of the world, to participate in new technologies and virtual spaces. The future of Indigenous languages is also in cyberspace, and we must begin to turn it into a fairer, more equal space for speakers of all the world's languages.

> *Let's tweet in Nahuatl, Mixe, Chinantec!!! New resources for strengthening languages…*
>
> 🅕 *20 July, 2011*

9 July, 2011

# EVERYDAY ACTION TO PROMOTE LINGUISTIC DIVERSITY FOR SPANISH SPEAKERS

The discrimination suffered by communities of Indigenous language speakers and the violation of their linguistic rights are systematic and have everyday consequences. The role of the monolingual Spanish-speaking community is crucial if we are to reverse, to some extent, the effects of forced Hispanicisation – of institutional discrimination against these languages. If your mother tongue is Spanish, there are many things you can do to help stop the violation of linguistic rights and thereby provide an opportunity to protect linguistic diversity. The greatest cause of language death is discrimination and violation of the rights of their speakers. Tackling

*Today, on the Day of the Musician, a beautiful tongue-twister in Ayuujk:*

*Xuujx xuxpë, xu'ukx xu'pxpë.*
*Xu'upxë xuujx, xu'ukx xuxpë.*
*Xuu'ux xu'kx, xu'pxpë ja xuxpë.*

*The musical instrument plays, the hummingbird takes a drink.*

*Take a drink, musical instrument, hummingbird will sing the tune.*

*The hummingbird sings a tune while the musician is taking a drink.*

*Juana Martínez*
*(Taken from Tajëëw Díaz Robles's wall).*

**f**  *22 Nov, 2011*

161

this through everyday action can be effective and enormously helpful. Here are some ideas:

a) Inform yourself and spread the word. The fact that most Mexicans cannot name the languages spoken in their country is a key indicator of the problem, and forms part of the campaign to make them disappear. Combat this by seeking information: do you know the names of the languages spoken in your state and country? Do you know the names of the linguistic families they belong to? Do you know the history of writing in those Indigenous languages? Share your knowledge of linguistic diversity with your family and friends.

b) Language, not dialect. Discrimination starts with naming. Indigenous languages are exactly that, languages, not dialects. If you know someone who uses the word dialect to name Indigenous languages, explain to them, very courteously, that that is not what they are.

 c) Join the cause. Unfortunately, in this country linguistic rights continue to be violated: speakers of Indigenous languages are denied the right to register their children with names in their languages, the judicial system and health system refuse them interpreters, many schools still forbid the use of these languages, the national press does not print content in Indigenous languages. Seek information about these specific cases and learn about them; help us denounce them and spread the word.

d) Visibilise. Do you have a new project? Are you launching a shop? A new product? Are you writing a book? Shooting a film? Buying a doll and looking for a name? Remember that there are words in hundreds of Mexican languages that could give a name to your new project. If you live in a multilingual country, you have multiple naming options that are also opportunities to disseminate other languages and linguistic diversity. There will always be someone who asks: what does that mean? what language is that? Take advantage of those moments.

> *There must be a word in some language for 'anticipatory nostalgia'…*
>
>   7 Aug, 2011

e) Include. If you work in a bakery, you can look up how to say 'happy birthday' in several Mexican languages and then suggest it to your customers buying birthday cakes. You can ask for signs in your workplace to appear in Indigenous languages: do you know how to say 'welcome' in Mixe? 'Ey ky mment.' If you work in an office that has over-the-counter service, you can, in addition to Spanish, use numbers written in a local Indigenous language for each window. Have a radio show? Include songs in different languages.

> *Just because you don't speak an Indigenous language doesn't mean you don't have linguistic rights.*
>
> 𝕏  13 April, 2013

f) Be demanding. You have the right to get to know and enjoy all of Mexico's national languages. For example, you could look up one of the many beautiful Indigenous names to call your child. This would help combat

> *In Mixe, 'to seal a document' is 'tsä'äy yë neky' – literally, 'to burn the paper' – and I guess it's a beautiful linguistic reminder of when they still used 'marcas de fuego', red-hot metal, to mark official documents…*
>
> 🌐  4 Jan, 2016

discrimination against these languages in public administration. You can arrange for your school or university to offer classes in one of the Indigenous languages in your local area. Ask for information about the country's languages to be included in a dignified way in curricula and in institutional publications.

g) Educate about diversity. There are many ways of getting your family involved in linguistic diversity. These include posters, games of bingo, bilingual books and films produced in Mexican languages other than Spanish.

h) Learn. 'Good morning' in Zoque. 'See you later' in Purépecha. 'Kiss me' in Mixe. A song in Nahuatl. A tongue twister in Valley Zapotec. How to count to ten in Cora. 'Moon' in Tepehua. Whatever you fancy.

> *Kajaanaxy y'uktuun muku'uktëjk, tëë ëjts yoo n'änmëjä'än kyätkën...*
>
> 🅕    *10 Oct, 2017*

> *'Friends, it's been raining so much I feel like my soul's getting mouldy.'*
>
> 🅕    *10 Oct, 2017*

Have other ideas for how to include linguistic diversity in your everyday life? Let us know.

15 Aug, 2015

# MAXU'NK: DUÉRMASE MI NIÑO, DUÉRMASEME YA

## LULLABIES IN LANGUAGES FROM AROUND THE WORLD

$S$ome Mixe communities believe new-borns arrive with a linguistic gift – they understand a universal language that will later be polished with adult words until it's turned into a perfect diamond: Ayuujk. In dreams, we sometimes remember the universal language we were born with – it's the language we use when we go mad or on our deathbeds. Words in that universal language reconnect us with the world of the dead, which is perhaps similar to the world of the not-yet-born, of the

*My penchant for drama didn't come from nowhere. This is what I used to listen to as a child, and though I didn't understand the lyrics back then, I definitely channelled their spirit, hahaha:* Quisiera abrir lentamente mis venas, mi sangre toda verterla a tus pies para poderte demostrar que más no puedo amar y entonces morir después... *[I'd like to slowly open my veins, spill all my blood at your feet to show you it's impossible to love you more than I do, and then to die...] (Javier Solís, 'Sombras nada más' [Just Shadows])*

**f** *1 June, 2011*

165

not-yet-conceived. Every culture has a different understanding of what language acquisition involves, and there are still heated debates between different scientific approaches to the phenomenon.

Babies' interaction with the world's languages begins before they're born: they can hear the language spoken by their mother and so, though *mother tongue* is not a synonym of *the mother's language*, there is an initial linguistic relationship between mother and child. It's no surprise, therefore, that words become incantations to stop the flow of tears, or to encourage sleep, bravery, or hope. Lullabies, which are transmitted mainly in the oral tradition, are a reflection in music and lyrics of different cultural approaches to infancy. Each culture uses lullabies for a different purpose: there is a lullaby in Seri, for example, that people sing not to rock or lull a child to sleep, or to get them to stop crying, but rather 'to inspire a fighting spirit in girls, so that when they grow up they'll know how to confront the world's problems', as the lyrics themselves tell us.

A lullaby is an oral text specifically composed to connect with people receiving the linguistic heritage of the culture into which they were born. Lullabies are linguistic buildings offered to the children learning to inhabit them. The words of lullabies can be directed at babies, or they can be linguistic formulae for attracting desirable attributes or destinies for new-borns.

In 2010, a couple set up a project called La Furgo-Nana. They travelled all over Latin America in a van (a 'furgoneta'), documenting the state of children's rights and lullabies in the different places they visited, some of them in languages other than Spanish.[15]

---

[15] The La Furgo-Nana website is no longer active, but you can consult their X, Facebook or YouTube channel instead.

Lullabies can be a way to expose babies to the diversity of languages in the world. In what follows, I present a short selection of lullabies in different languages to send children to sleep and inspire courage in them: because sleep and courage know no linguistic boundaries.

 Otomi. Oto-Manguean family. 'Hyadi. Canción de cuna (Letra en Otomí).'

Toba. Mataco-Guaicuru family. Spoken in Argentina: 'Tonolec – Canción de Cuna / Lullaby.'

 Seri: 'Nana Conca'ac (Seri) 1.'

English. Indo-European family: 'Yo-Yo Ma & Bobby McFerrin – Hush Little Baby.'

 Nahuatl. Uto-Aztecan family: 'Canción de cuna en lengua Nahuatl.'

Lakota. Siouan family.

 Mixtec. Oto-Manguean family. (Thanks to Avelardo Moctezuma for introducing me to this song): 'Canto mixteco para dormir, aaron arias, erick de jesus.'

Sephardi. Indo-European family. (Thanks to  Manuel Domingo for introducing me to this song): 'ANA ALCAIDE: DURME DURME –Sinagoga del Tránsito de Toledo.'

20 May, 2015

# ROCK IN YOUR LANGUAGE: MULTILINGUAL JUKEBOX

*En lo puro no hay futuro*
*la pureza está en la mezcla*
*en la mezcla de lo puro*
*que antes que puro fue mezcla*

*[There's no future in the pure*
*purity lies in the mix*
*in the mix of the pure*
*which before it was pure was a mix]*
Jarabe de Palo[16]

...**a**nd reggae, cumbia, ballads, rap, ska, and other music in your language – in Mixe, Maya, Seri, Nahuatl, Huichol, and a huge range of other tongues.

Scandalised individuals who complain of a loss of identity, of cultural corruption or undesirable contamination, can do very little about the new music emerging from interesting combinations of rhythms, traditions and Indigenous languages in Mexico. On the contrary, Maya rap, Tzotzil, Seri and Nahua rock, Huichol cumbia and

[16] I owe this quotation (one of my favourites), for which I am grateful, to my friend Francisco Arellanes.

Mixe reggae are emerging as a sign of reaffirmation: a form of resistance which, as Sheba Camacho puts it, is not politicised and can therefore be much more effective in new contexts.

It's true that Indigenous peoples' musical traditions, which can be very different from one another, constitute a hugely important legacy, but the existence of intercultural dialogues in music doesn't deny that heritage – new mash-ups don't pose a threat to tradition, but rather offer a way of experiencing and entering into dialogue with it. The greatest threat to traditional music isn't that it's being mixed, rather, it's being forgotten.

*Kastiixy pat'ajtsp: the lovely tradition of dancing a Mixe fandango under the firework tower, to the beat of the philharmonic bands.*
*#CelebrationIsResistance*
*#HighlandLove*

29 Jan, 2017

I don't agree with the false opposition set up to categorically divide traditional and modern music. Traditional music alive today is as modern as can be, precisely because it's alive. In the case of Mixe, for example, the sound of a wind ensemble, which is paradigmatic of the tradition, is still enjoyed and still meaningful today, and it's the same generation that sings reggae in Mixe that also composes new pieces.

What we consider 'traditional' and 'authentic' is a matter of perspective: the first time I heard 'Yesterday' I was a little girl. It was an unforgettable version played by the 'traditional' Tlahuitoltepec Mixe philharmonic band at a celebration in my hometown; the day I heard the Beatles playing it, I was completely taken aback, thrilled to know that a 'traditional' piece by the Mixe wind ensembles had had so much reach that a band in a far-off country had adapted it and given it lyrics in English. I still find it hard not to feel like 'Yesterday' by the Beatles is a cover of a piece belonging to the Ayuujk musical tradition.

To go back to new music, it's fascinating to see the genres chosen for new songs in different Indigenous languages. Perhaps it's my own ignorance, but I'm yet to hear a pasito duranguense in a Mexican language other than Spanish, though there are plenty of examples of rock songs. What does this preference for certain musical genres say about the movement in which they're used, a movement seeking to reclaim Indigenous cultures?

When it comes to distribution and reception, the situation is unique. It speaks volumes that all you need to do is turn on the radio to realise that, apart from a growing number of community radio stations, it's almost impossible to tune into a station where you can hear music that reflects the diversity of languages spoken in our country. And so national radio stations are added to the blacklist of spaces where linguistic diversity is gagged. It seems a far-off dream for the music industry to be sensitive to the linguistic reality in which it operates and produces. Fortunately, the internet facilitates free exchange and means we don't have to depend so much on record labels and music shops. I once heard someone argue that they don't record or promote groups that sing in languages other than Spanish because, as they saw it, people were frustrated by not being able to understand the lyrics; any non-English speaker who has enjoyed songs in English will know how poor an argument this is.

Meanwhile, music festivals rarely include music that's linguistically diverse. The most we can boast are spaces exclusive to music in Indigenous languages, removed from the context of music production in Mexico today. One example is the KasahastVanut Contemporary Indigenous Music Festival organised by the National Commission for the Development of Indigenous Communities – a good place to start to learn about this topic.

The music increasingly produced in this country's Indigenous languages, in a range of genres, reflects a complex reality that belies the simple categorisation Indigenous peoples are subjected to almost everywhere. It often responds to the phenomenon of migration, or to pleasure and dialogue between cultures. In my experience, most people involved in creating this music form part of intensive movements to reclaim culture; this might seem like a contradiction, but of course it isn't. In the light of this phenomenon, rock seems more useful to the Indigenous movement than purist discourses that deny exchange and contact as essential characteristics of all peoples of the world.

*My name is Andrea Isabel Ixchíu Hernández and I am K'iché. I play the drums and I sing. I was in a rock band once. I like grunge, punk, grindcore, metal. Rock and roll led me to work as a land defender. I grew up in a collective, communal environment where service and protest were important. And now I'm in charge of the forest. A month ago, when I turned 24, the municipality of Totonicapán's Urban Area 2, where I live, put me in charge of overseeing the Board of Directors of Natural Resources. My mission is to protect this place for a year. It's a great honour and a great responsibility. Mainly because it's the first time in history that this Indigenous organisation has given the presidency to a young, female rock fan.'[17]*

       *12 July, 2015*

[17] Andrea Ixchíu is a K'iché woman from Totonicapán, Guatemala. She is a Human Rights defender and a Community Communicator who devotes herself to promoting the rights of Indigenous women in Guatemala. Since she was a child, Andrea has been organising local campaigns to denounce violence against women in her community. She now offers workshops to young people on how to prevent gender-based violence.

I also believe music can be a great medium for getting more people to enjoy multilingualism; it's better to build bridges through the medium of music: the road is wider and there are lanes in both directions. After all, it's easier to open your mind once you've opened your ears.

*MULTILINGUAL JUKEBOX*

In what follows, I present a sample of music from different genres in some of Mexico's languages. The sample makes no attempt to be representative, much less exhaustive: let's just say I'd like to share some of the linguistically diverse music in my listening life, a small sample that is inevitably biased towards Mixe, for obvious reasons I hope you'll understand. They appear here in no particular order. There are, I'm sure, unforgivable omissions that are proof of my ignorance: let this serve as an invitation to share in a search that's only just begun.

> *It would seem the Mexican state only feels comfortable establishing a relationship with Indigenous peoples through folklore.*
>
> X                    *19 July, 2013*

REGGAE IN MIXE:

 Rockdrigo Vargas, a Tlahuitoltepec Mixe, who currently lives in California.

ROCK IN TZOTZIL:

 Sak Tzevul ('lightning-thunder') is a well-known, pioneering band, formed in 1996. I recommend searching online for some of their excellent tracks.

## BALLADS IN MIXE:

 Javier Gil hails from Ayutla Mixe. As well as being a singer and composer, he teaches music to children, placing emphasis on linguistic diversity.

## CUMBIA IN HUICHOL:

 El venado azul ('The Blue Deer'): a band from the Sierra Madre Occidental in Jalisco state. They have toured the country with their 'Cumbia Cusinela' (whose lyrics are controversial, it has to be said) and performed at Wirikuta Fest.

There's a version sung by one of the band member's sons, as well as an original version with lyrics.

## MIXE FUSION:

 I'll be honest, I don't really know how to define this musical genre. The fascinating Banda Región Mixe de Tlahuitoltepec fuses traditional wind music with new elements taken from other traditions. The musicians were trained in the Ayuujk musical tradition but seek out new musical discourses. Several of their pieces are in Mixe.

## ROCK IN SERI:

 Hamac Caziim ('Divine Fire') is a Seri group from Sonora who formed in 1995. They have had a long career and are known both locally and nationally. Their music has taken them to different parts of the country as well as abroad.

## SOPRANO IN MIXE:

 The Mixe soprano Marí Reyna González is a native Tlahuitoltepec Mixe who is studying singing in Guadalajara and in November this year (2013) performed in the Teatro Juárez in Oaxaca City.

## RAP AND HIP-HOP IN MAYA:

 Pat Boy is from Quintana Roo and has a very interesting repertoire. In the QR code there's an interview and a video where you can learn more.

## ROCK IN NAHUATL:

 And to top off this musical feast, how about a Nahuatl version of 'Sabotage' by the Beastie Boys? In Arreola+Carballo, Mexican rock stars Alonso and Chema Arreola join forces with writer and communicator Mardonio Carballo to explore creatively in Nahuatl.

So that's it, an invitation: there is plenty to listen to, plenty to explore.

8 May, 2013

# WRITTEN LANDSCAPES

$B$ack when I first started paying attention to writing, everything around me was embroidered with letters representing a language I didn't speak yet: letters on posters welcoming people to the town celebration, letters on the sign outside the municipal offices, letters on the packaging of the Motitas chewing gum from my childhood and the letters I was learning to trace, trembling, in my first notebook. They all represented words in Spanish, only Spanish, and perhaps a few in English.

In public spaces I never saw words written in the language I actually spoke. Specialists in literacy maintain, or at least this is what I've understood, that literacy begins at the very moment we're invaded by written stimuli; the moment we begin to be inundated by letters, not the moment we learn to decode them, not the moment when we begin to read or write. Literacy begins when we see ourselves in a sea of letters, when written landscapes stretch out before us.

We live in lettered environments: milk cartons, road signs, advertising, place names. All form part of the written

> *Jä'äy' and 'jä'äy' are homophonic in Ayutla Mixe: the noun 'person' and the verb 'to write'.*
>
> 𝕏                    *18 Mar, 2014*

landscape, except this landscape can only be observed through Spanish lenses. In most communities where an Indigenous language is spoken, the written landscape rarely includes the mother tongue of most of its inhabitants; it would be as if in Mexico City all the writing, from the label on a fizzy drink bottle to the advertising on the motorway, were in German rather than Spanish. There are few places where the unequal relationship between Mexico's languages is more evident. A single language floods the written landscape, no matter which part of the country you are in; only one language can be codified in graphemes, letters, alphabets.

To develop writing in many Indigenous languages we need to seek a more balanced written landscape, the landscape of letters seen on a daily basis. To acquire literacy in our languages, people must be able to produce words in their mother tongue from their environment; they must receive visual and written stimuli not just in Spanish. The language represented in the written landscape acquires huge symbolic value, and respect for the diversity of languages must involve better representation in the realm of letters and written symbols. Balancing the written landscape in communities that speak an Indigenous language and cities where many languages are spoken is crucial work. I hope that in the city of Oaxaca public spaces will

*Ñu York!!*
*(As, according to Zaidee, a friend of a friend says about the fact so many Mixtecan languages are spoken there).*

 4 Oct, 2011

*The fact that I learned to read in Spanish and not in my mother tongue must in some way have determined my relationship with written language. I will never have the experience of becoming literate in Ayuujk, though I have now learned to write it.*

 12 Sept, 2012

soon have more written elements in Valley Zapotec as well as in Spanish and English.

The written landscape in Indigenous communities is gradually beginning to change; for example, in Ayutla, my hometown, the names of streets and paths are now written and numbered in Mixe. Thanks to the efforts of a group of community members, my town is starting, little by little, to even out the written landscape to which we're exposed. The Mixe signs now found on practically every house have provoked a huge range of reactions, among which the most important, in my opinion, is that the topic is talked about more now – our language's writing and letters are now discussed. Young children will grow up with a better idea than I had at their age: they'll know early on that Mixe can be written down and used in public spaces. Now I just hope the authorities issuing documents bearing official addresses will register street names in Ayuujk. All being well, my next polling card will show my address as Konk käm'äm 48 jëxtijkxy tyuktujk. I'll leave it here, in case one day you want to come and visit me.

17 July, 2013

# THE DELICACIES OF THE
# POST-BABEL WORLD

Learning other languages is one of the most obvious ways of enjoying the world's linguistic diversity. The human brain has an amazing capacity to learn new languages, and in great numbers. To achieve this, you need either to be exposed, for many possible reasons, to a multilingual environment, or else to have a peculiar passion for learning new languages. To illustrate the first case, I can think of the example of the extraordinary musician Mali Ali Farka Touré and all the languages he mastered while working as a travelling salesman. I would almost put money on his polyglot brain having subtly but convincingly influenced the way he composed and played his extraordinary music (you can enjoy, for example, a wonderful piece called 'Talking Timbuktu' on YouTube).

As for the second case, the perfect example: the poet and translator Enrique Servín from Chihuahua, a polyglot writer and translator who could hold conversations in meticulous Tarahumara and who translated from Arabic, Nahuatl and Russian. I was so sorry to hear about the heart attack that took the life of this man who was more committed than almost anybody to this country's Indigenous languages. (If you'd like to learn more about him, I recommend the interview with him in *Tierra Adentro*.)

Learning another language gives the mind the gift of linguistic ubiquity. It's an enjoyable process in which the masses of sound that at first comprise an unknown language are transformed into an edifice of meaning and sense that we can walk through, decorate and furnish, until we're able to inhabit it comfortably. To learn many languages is to build multiple homes for our thoughts.

There exist, however, other ways of enjoying the delights offered by the post-Babel world. You can eat entire delicious linguistic cakes, or you can just have a slice of one, pick a little at another, satisfy yourself with the crumbs of a third or have nothing but the cherry on the top of that pistachio cake which, although delicious, you're too full to eat. This is the idea underlying a proposal known as language awareness, which I heard about from the linguist Michel Launey, and which we could say is a kind of invitation not only to be aware of but also to enjoy linguistic diversity itself – to be open and awake to it.

*Conversations with my grand-mother (part one):*
G: *Yakxon nnaykyo'ok*
Me: ¿*Jatii?*
G: *Tek amëjë'n mnaya'pta'aky*
PLOP.

𝕏                   *8 Jan, 2012*

There are many ways to find this enjoyment, and to different degrees. Think, for example, of a woman who speaks Zoque and Spanish as mother tongues, who then learns Tojolabal and English fluently as second languages, then later decides to learn

Russian so she can understand a Chekhov story in the original. While doing all this, she learns to sing a couple of songs in Zapotec from Teotitlán del Valle that she thinks are beautiful, a girlfriend teaches her to say 'I miss you' in Tzotzil and then, while travelling, she's taught to count to twenty in Tarahumara. In addition to all this, she knows the names of the language families spoken in her country, can say hello in Chol, a few curious words in Japanese, and can name the planet Venus in Mixe.

*Pä'ämkukäjpxëp is more or less the equivalent of Orion's belt.*

X                    *29 Nov, 2014*

There are many ways we can get involved with the world's languages. They enrich us and teach us that each of them contains something valuable, which in the long term generates greater possibilities for dialogue and for understanding others, the many other people out there. We can decide to what extent languages form part of our knowledge of the world.

A quality education should allow for these various ways of encountering languages, which live, exist and, at the end of the day, are part of our world heritage, insofar as they are products of our species. As humans we can enjoy them, speak them, read them, learn them, even if that means only a handful of words or just knowing of their existence and location in the country where we live.

To begin, I want to list a few titbits to whet your appetites for the languages of Mexico. You decide which cake and how much of it you'd like to eat. Want to learn to speak Maya? Nahuatl? Learn how to count in Zapotec? Say 'you're beautiful' in Mixe? Sing a song in Purépecha? The possibilities are infinite.

There's an episode of Sesame Street available in Nahuatl on YouTube.[18]

Did you know that speakers of Chinantec, a tonal language, can have entire conversations by whistling the tones of words?

Want to flick through a reprint of *Arte de la lengua zapoteca* (Art of the Zapotec Language) by Fray Juan de Córdova? The first edition of this grammar is from 1578, eight years before  the first English grammar was published.[19]

Want to sing happy birthday in Otomi?

Want to learn to count to twenty in Tzotzil?

The possibilities are almost infinite.

4 June, 2014

---

[18] The title of the YouTube video is 'Plaza Sésamo en Nahuatl / subtítulos en español'. The information below explains that 'In 2011 Sesame Street Workshop authorised INALI to make Sesame Street in Nahuatl (a single episode) with the aim of disseminating it in Nahuatl-speaking communities, as a sample of alternative programming of educational content in Indigenous languages.'
[19] For the re-edition mentioned here, see Córdova, J., *Arte del idioma zapoteco* (Morelia: Imprenta del Gobierno, 1886).

# SPEECH AS AN ACT OF RESISTENCE: JAMYATS

Every time you speak in one of this country's Indigenous languages, every time you start a conversation in Seri, every time a thought forms in the grammatical structures of Zoque, it's an act of resistance. What are we resisting? We're resisting orchestrated forced Hispanicisation campaigns. We're saying 'you were not enough' to the budget spent on programmes, teachers and books that repeatedly told us we couldn't speak in the languages of our communities. We're resisting all government efforts, throughout the history of Mexico as a country, to eliminate our languages.

Every time we hold an assembly in Mixtec to discuss matters of public life in our community, we're saying to the Mexican state that we do not accept Spanish as the only language, the de facto official language. When we

*We are memory and our superpower is remembering.*

*26 Nov, 2016*

*Great news!!! A second woman has been elected municipal president through community assembly in the Mixe region. No doubt about it, for a while now women's intense participation in community life has been reflected more and more in elections as they serve in different roles.*

*10 Sept, 2011*

buy and sell goods in the market in Chatino, we're telling the world that despite the fines, the beatings, being caned on our hands, the physical punishment, we'd rather do mental arithmetic in our own language.

Every time you try to learn an Indigenous language, you're saying to the state that even though it doesn't provide you with the spaces in which to do so, you wish, as is your right, to travel to other cognitive territories – territories that the state is trying to eliminate.

Every time I talk to a small child in Mixe, every time I tell them stories, I'm saying to the Mexican state that, despite all its efforts to the contrary, I can still find ways to pass on the language. Every time you give your daughter an Indigenous name, a name written with diereses, apostrophes, or accents, you are telling the system that you're willing to suffer the torment they'll subject you to if only they would understand, once and for all, that all it would take is to programme the computers to accept those characters, which are not foreign, and that you have rights.

*I speak Mixe to see if I can forget the national anthem.*

X                    *12 Jan, 2015*

*I speak Mixe as an attack on national 'identity'.*

X                    *12 Jan, 2015*

At the beginning of Mexico's life as an independent country, approximately 65% of the population spoke one of its Indigenous languages. Today, there are only 6.5% of us. Every time we utter a speech act in one of the country's Indigenous languages, every sentence sends the message that we're resisting, that we're still here, that we're still talking and that our voices take shape through syntactic structures and semantic systems that make defenders of the state nervous.

We might not realise it, but every time we debate in Zapotec, Mayo or Maya, we escape state-manipulated, state-controlled discourses, because it simply does not understand us. The upside of the battle that's been waged against Indigenous languages is that the state, because of its rejection of and resistance to them, cannot appropriate these linguistic territories.

Every time you speak an Indigenous language, you are resisting. To speak an Indigenous language in the present circumstances is to inhabit a cognitive territory that has not been conquered yet, or at least not completely. Let's escape to those territories, let's inhabit them. Remember this whenever you speak: jamyats, ejtp.

17 July, 2015

𝕏 18 Sept, 2018

COLMIX is a collective of young Mixes to which I am very proud to belong; and we have our own webpage! **https://colmix.org/**

---

𝕏 10 Jan, 2018

I hang out most days with a toddler who speaks Ayuujk.
I ask her:
-**¿Maxu'nk mëjts, këteea?**
She replies:
- **Ka't, ëjts Nutsy.**
And my heart melts.

𝕏 13 July, 2017

25 days without drinking water in my community. An armed group is hijacking our spring. WHO ARMED THEM? 1 man dead, 7 people injured, 4 women kidnapped.

---

𝕗 12 April, 2016

The joys, the heartaches, the marvels, the desperation, the miracles, the conflicts and the things to be learned from living in a community that prioritises consensus.

X  10 Feb, 2015

# Did you know that in Matlatzinca there are four ways of saying 'we'? That there are two in Mixe and only one in Spanish?

---

X  2 July, 2016

**You, me, rolling in each other's arms in this meadow full of flowers on our ranch in Ayutla. I don't know, think about it.** #HighlandLove

X  15 Feb, 2020

I feel like I'm going to devote the rest of my life to remembering the part of it I shared with my grandmother.

# SPEECH TO THE CHAMBER OF DEPUTIES

The original recording of Yásnaya's speech can be found on YouTube.

# NËWEMP, JA NËËJ JËTS JA ÄÄ AYUUJK

May Nëwemp xyëë tmëët mëte'ep ka't yak'ejx. Nëwemp. Nëëj wemp. Ayuujk. Giajmïï. Nëëjkëjxp. Chinanteco ää. Nangi ndá. Ja nääjx mëte'ep nëëjetpy ejtp. Mazateco ää Kuríhi. Nëëjetpy. Chichimeco ää Nu koyo. Nek käjp. Mixteco ää Jayeen ojts yä'ät käjp te'n yakxëmo'oy. Jatëkoojk yä'ät et mëte'ep tsyäm tu'uk ja ana'amën tnëtë-naapy: Nëwemp. ¿Tii te'n nëëjetpy ja Nëwemp yyi'tspy' Tu'uk majkts Ayuujk yä'ät xëë nnëmatyä'äkä'än ¿Jatii ku ää Ayuujk kyutëkeenyët? Tsyäm, jawaan kyamäjk-möjkxmo'ony ja ää ja Ayuujk tëkatsyety yakkajpxy yää et nääjxwiiny. Ja Catalogue of Endangered Languages te'ep jam ejtp mää ja Hawaii University tnëkäjpxp ku katëkëëk po'ety tu'uk ja ää Ayuujk jyëntëkey, tu'uk ää Ayuujk y'ameny, tu'uk ää Ayuujk y'ooky. Ja UNESCO nayte'n tnëkajpxy ku ja tu'uk mëke'pxy jëmëëjt tëë näjty kyutëkeenyët jawaan ka kujkwa'kxy ja ää Ayuujk mëte'epety tsyäm yakkäjpx. Tam jënë'n ja jujky'äjtën nyaxy, nijuunëm ijty te'n kyajaty, kyakupety ku maynaxy ja ää ja Ayuujk kyutëkey ¿Jatii ku tsyäm jëte'n kanääknaxy ja ää ja Ayuujk y'o'knët?

Jawaan kyatëkëëk mëke'pxy jemëëjt ku ja et nääxwy'nyët ojts okwä'äny wya'kxy, ja tsäwä'än ojts ja et nääxwyi'nyët takwa'kxy. Wa'kxy ja et nääjwiiny ojts tyany. Ka't jatu'uk et nääjxwi'inyët mnäxt pën ka't ja neky xmëët. Jawaan kyamajstmëke'pxy ja ana'amën kutujkën ojts tu'uk tu'uk apiky y'ëjxta'aky. Katu'uk ja ana'amën, ja jëntsën tmëët'ät jëts tu'uk ja'y ja wet te'ep jyëntsë'ëjkëtëp katu'ukety, tu'uk ja jënmä'äny ja'y takmëjtëkët, tu'uk ja'y ja tsënääyën ja tënä'äyën tkupëkt, jëts nayte'n tu'uk ja'y ja ää ja Ayuujk ojts taktsopäätt. Ja ää Ayuujk te'ep ka't ja jëntsëntëjk taktunt ka't ja tsyoopaty, yak'apajxp ja', yak'ëjxwejtsp ja'.

Myajktsmëke'pxy jëmëjtëp ojts tsyonta'aky yä'ät ana'amën mëte'ep tsyäm Nëwemp txëë'äjtp. Tëkëëk mëke'pxy jëmëjt näjty tëë nyäjxn ku te'n ojts ja amaxän jä'äy jyä'ät, ja 1820 jëts 65 ka tu'uk mëke'pxyety ijty jä'äy ja kyë'm ää Ayuujk tkajpxy, ää Ayuujk te'ep jëti'myëm ejtp, men pat, yää yakkäjpxp. Nëwaan ijty ja jä'äy te'ep amaxän tkäjpxtëpp. Tsyäm, ku majtskmëke'pxy jëmëëjt tëë nyaxy, 6.5 ka tu'uk mëke'pxyety ja'y ja kë'm y'ää y'Ayuujk tjaa'akkäjpxp. Amaxän tëë takmëjtëkët. Myajtskmëke'pxy jëmëjtëp ëëts n'ää n'Ayuujk ijty jawan kajaa yakkäjpxp, ja Nahuatl, ja Maya, ja Mayo, ja tepehua, ja tepehuano, ja Ayuujk jëts jënë'n ja patkëmët Ayuujk na'amuk. Nëwaan ijty ja amaxän jä'äy yää. Kumajtsk mëke'pxy jëmëjt, tsyäm, tëë kajaa ëëts ja n'ää n'Ayuujk xak'ëjxnëjkxt.

¿Xë'n ojts xtunt jëts xakkutëkeety?

¿Ey'äjtën te'n. ja'y. ëëts ja n'ää n'Ayuujk nmastutnëta? Ka't, ka't jyëte'n. Te'nte'n ojts ttanëpëtääkët pënety Nëwemp ojts y'ana'amt, ku ka't ëëts ja n'ää ja n'Ayuujk tsyoopääty, ku ja'y amaxän yakkäjpxt. Taa te'n ëëts nteetymä'äy ntääkmä'äy yakwopt, yak'ojt, yak'apaxt ku y'ää y'Ayuujk tkäjpxt. "Ka't yë tsyoopääty" te'n ojts yaknëëjmët. "Nëwempët jä'äy mejts, amaxän te'n ja'y mkäjpxt, jatyëkey yë m'ää m'Ayuujk" te'n ojts yaknëëjmët. Kajaa te'n ojts ja tunk taktuyo'oty, kajaa te'n ojts nya'atsipyët jëts te'n ëëts naktakuwän'ät ja amaxän, jëts ëëts ja nkë'm ää Ayuujk njatyëke'etyët. Ja ëjxpëjktääjk ojts kajaa ëëts ja n'Ayuujk ojts tjo'otsy. Nëwemp ëëts ja n'ää n'Ayuujk tëë xpëjkxyët. Ja nëëj ëjts xpatamtëp, xjo'tstëp, xak'amontëp. Ey ja anä'ämën nekyetpy tëë jyatëkatsy, ti'nyëm ëëts ja n'ää n'Ayuujk yak'apexy, ti'nyëm yak'ëjxwitsy. Ka't ëëts n'ää n'Ayuujk yakmëjpëkta'aky mää ëjxpëjktääjkën, ni ka't mää jä'äy yaknëpa'ayo'oyën, ni ka't mää jä'äy nyaytseyët. Ka't ëëts n'ää n'Ayuujk kë'm kyutëkey, yakkutëkeetyëp ojts.

Yakkutëketyëp nayte'n ku ëëts ja n'et ja nnääjx-wiiny ka't tjëntsë'ëkët, ku ëëts ja n'et ja nääjxwiiny ja'y tnëtookt, ku ka't ëëts yakxon ka'pxy, tam tyu'ntët, xakkäjpxt pën ntajotkujk'äjtëp ëëts ku ja tunk te'ep meets nmjënmaatyëp tyu'uyo'oty mää ëëts n'et nnääjx-wi'nyët. Yakkutëkeetyëp nayte'n ëëts n'ää n'Ayuujk ku ëëts ja nmuku'uktëjk xak'ookt, ja nmuku'uk te'ep ëëts ja n'et nnääjxwi'nyët nyëkuwäntutëp tam te'n jënë'n men pat jyatyën.

¿Xë'n ëëts ja n'ää n'Ayuujk myëjët myayët ku ëëts ja nmuku'uk ja'y tak'ookt, tak'amont, takjëntëkeety? ¿Xë'n ëëts ja n'ää n'Ayuujk myëjët myayët ku ëëts ja n'et ka't yakjëntsë'ëk? Te'nte'n ëëts jam tsyäm njätt nkëpatt. Jam tsyäm ëjts nkäjpotp. Tukyo'm, Wäjkwemp ka't nëëj tee. Jawaan kyamajtskjëmëëjt ku ëëts ja nëëj nakpëëjkët jëts tsyämnëm ka't ëëts pën xnëpayo'oyy, ey jënë'n ëëts tëë nja'ëëny, njanëkajpxy ku ëëts ja nëëj nakpëjkët, ey ëëts naky'ijxy ku jajp ja tiiy'äjtën yakmëët. Pujx, tujn, pujxpäjk, ja' te'n yaktuntëp jëts ëëts ja nëëj nakpëjkët, ku ja nëëmu'uty tak'amont, ey ja neky ja tiiy'äjtën tjayaky ku ka't kyutiky ku pën nëëj mpëjkxët, ku pën kutë'ëts maktanët. Ka't ëëts nnëëj yukjä'tn jëts kajaa y'ayoot ja mëjjä'ätyëk, ja mutsk anä'äjk. Ja et nääjxwyi'nyët, ja nëëj, ja xoj, ja' te'n ää Ayuujk tyajujky'atpy.

¿Xë'n te'n ja ää ja Ayuujk myayët?

Ka't ëëts n'ää n'Ayuujk kyutëkeyy. Yakkutëkeetyëp.
Nëwemp ëëts n'ää n'Ayuujk tëë takkyutëkeyy. Ja tu'mtsy
jënmä'äny, ja tu'mtsy ana'amën, tam nëëjën, te'ep jo'tsp.

# MEXICO:
# THE WATER AND THE WORD

Mexico and its many hidden names.

Nëwemp. In the place of water. Mixe.

Giajmïï. On the water. Chinantec.

Nangi ndá. Land amid the water. Mazatec.

Kuríhi. In the water. Chichimeca.

Nu koyo. Humid village. Mixtec.

These are the names that were given to this city. Then later to this state, the Mexican state: Mexico. What are the waters of Nëwemp hiding?

I'd like to offer a few ideas and to try and answer a question. Why are languages dying? There are currently around six thousand languages in the world. The University of Hawaii's Catalogue of Endangered Languages reports that, on average, every three months a language dies somewhere. UNESCO also reports that, within a hundred years, approximately half the languages currently spoken around the world will be extinct.

Never before in history has this happened. Never before have so many languages died out. Why are they dying now? About three hundred years ago, the world began to divide itself up and establish internal borders. The world was carved up and it was no longer possible to travel to other places without documentation. The world was carved up into approximately two hundred states or countries, each of them with a government, a flag to which they pay homage, a preferred mode of thinking, an accepted culture and, in order to construct this internal homogeneity, a single language that was assigned value as the language of the state. Languages other than the language of state and government were discriminated against and suppressed.

Two hundred years ago, the state now known as Mexico was established. Three hundred years after the Spanish conquest, in 1820, 65% of the population spoke an Indigenous language. Spanish was a minority language when the Mexican state was created. Today, only 6.5% are speakers of an Indigenous language, while Spanish has become dominant. Two hundred years ago, our languages were majority languages: Nahuatl, Maya, Mayo, Tepehua, Tepehuán, Mixe, and all other Indigenous languages. In two hundred years our languages have been minoritised.

How did they become minoritised? Did we suddenly decide to abandon our languages? That's not what happened. There was a process, driven by government policy, that devalued our languages in favour of just one, Spanish. For our languages to disappear, our ancestors had to endure beatings, reprimands and discrimination for speaking their mother tongues. 'Your language is worthless', they were repeatedly told. 'If you want to be a Mexican citizen you must speak the national language, Spanish. Stop using your own language,' they were told over and over again. The state made considerable efforts to enforce Hispanicisation with the end goal of eradicating our languages, especially from the school system. It was Mexico that took our languages from us, the water of its name washing us away, silencing us. Even now that the law has been changed, our languages are still discriminated against in the education system, the justice system and the health system. Our languages are not dying out by themselves; our languages are being killed.

Our languages are killed when our territories aren't respected, when our land is sold and concessions are granted, when consultations on whether or not we want projects carried out on our land aren't conducted as they should be.

Our languages are killed when our land defenders are murdered, as has been happening since time immemorial.

How can we strengthen our languages when those who speak them are being killed, silenced and disappeared? How can our words flourish in territories that are being plundered?

This is exactly what's happening in my community, Ayutla Mixe, in Oaxaca. We have no water. Two years ago, armed groups took possession of the spring from which we have historically drawn water and we still have not seen justice done, despite reporting the issue and demonstrating the rightness of our claim. The spring was taken from us by force, with weapons and bullets; by force, our source of water was taken from us, silenced. Despite the law saying that water is a human right, for two years we've had no water in our homes, which has had a disproportionate impact on children and old people.

It's the earth, the water and the trees that nourish the existence of our languages. How can our language be revitalised if our territory is under constant attack?

Our languages aren't dying, they're being killed. The Mexican state has blotted them out. A single way of thinking, a single culture, this single state, is washing them away with the water it's named after.

26 Feb, 2019

To protest a year of water shortages and lack of justice, instead of arming itself, my community took up musical instruments and played a funeral march in protest. Music, not bullets. I'm moved to think that Ayutla is my home.

Whenever thinking too much gets me down, feeling cures me; whenever feeling too much gets me down, thinking cures me…

# Because the milpa isn't a cornfield.

The furthest from the Mexican state I've ever lived is in my hometown: @AyutlaMixe.

# The etymology of the Mixe word në'ëjpy ('blood') is 'red water', perhaps that's why when we bleed 'we rain'.

---

**𝕗 11 Jan, 2017**

**You, me, in the mountains in winter, looking out at our field of flowering peach trees; I don't know, think about it... #HighlandLove**

𝕏 30 Oct, 2014

That relentless cold breeze promising the approach of Day of the Dead? **My grandmother says: 'It's the breath of our ancestors on their way.'**

# A RETURN VISIT: EPILOGUE

In October 2011 I received an invitation from Paola Quintanar Zárate, digital editor of *Este País* magazine, to write a weekly blog on topics relating to Indigenous languages and linguistic diversity. I'd never published anything outside of academic spaces and it seemed like a good opportunity to talk about something that had been keeping me up at night: the disappearance of linguistic diversity around the world. With a few brief interruptions, I've been publishing in that space ever since – a space that's given me the opportunity to learn a huge amount and to have conversations that would never have taken place in other circumstances. I'm deeply grateful not only to Paola Quintanar for the initial opportunity, but also to editors Jessica Pérez Casarrubias, María José Ramírez and Karen Villeda, who have been generous and patient with me along the way.

I'm also enormously grateful to Ana Aguilar Guevara, Julia Bravo Varela, Gustavo Ogarrio Badillo and Valentina Quaresma Rodríguez for carefully choosing a selection of those texts for the publisher Almadía, who took a chance on this book. It's thanks to their work that I can now revisit words written several years ago. This return visit has spurred me to write a few brief observations for this English language edition.

When we re-read our own work, we risk not recognising ourselves, or seeing undesirable versions of ourselves reflected back. Before revisiting these texts, I was worried I'd find serious discrepancies in this material written so long ago, but I also understood that I could never have arrived at my current thinking without the reflective journey involved in writing those earlier pieces. I know there's a risk that in a few years' time I'll read what I'm writing now through a new lens, and I suppose this compounds the idea that we never finish reflecting on and finding new approaches to the topics we're passionate about; our conclusions will always be, at best, provisional. I also wonder, now that there is to be a new edition in English, what interest these texts, written in my particular context, might hold for English-speaking readers. That said, I'm enthusiastic to think of the possible conversations these ideas might generate in other realities, given the current ideological weight of the English language in the context of linguistic diversity. There are similarities among all experiences of linguistic discrimination, even if the contexts where they take place are distant from one another; linguistic diversity is present all over the world. As far as I have observed, the English-speaking world has often seen Latin America as just that – a latinised territory where only languages such as Spanish and Portuguese are spoken. I hope this book will break with that prejudice and make clear that our territories – just like countries where English is the language of the state – are rich with linguistic diversity. And as I write these lines, I'm also reminded of immigrants to the United States who, because of linguistic discrimination, never had the chance to inherit the Indigenous language of their ancestors' countries of origin, or indeed Castilian, because of the same linguistic violence. I'm pleased to think that I can now connect with those people through

English, thanks to Ellen Jones's meticulous translation work, which allows me to cross those linguistic bridges. Tyoskujuyëp, as we say in Ayuujk, to Charco Press for taking a chance on this book.

The following is a reflection, of sorts, prompted by the re-reading of my own texts.

## CELEBRATING DIVERSITY

I am surprised today, just as I was the day when I published my first blog entry, by the obvious but astonishing fact that so many languages exist in the world: I'm surprised that they're so different and at the same time so similar. That said, my initial enchantment with language diversity and its importance has transformed over time into a more specific concern for the political, economic and social conditions of the people who speak the world's most vulnerable languages. I care about languages now just as much as I cared about them almost twelve years ago, but now I'm more interested in their speakers. After finishing my masters in linguistics, I was able to recognise very specific grammatical phenomena, but I knew nothing about basic aspects of linguistic diversity in this country. That knowledge was acquired in other spaces, through working directly with communities of speakers of different languages. In my earliest publications, my approach to these topics was motivated by enthusiastic naivety. I was under the impression that celebrating diversity could help people value it more highly and therefore slow down language death. I still consider this important, because we cannot value what we know nothing about, but I think I've begun to reflect more on the urgency of creating spaces of linguistic resistance, and to analyse factors intrinsically linked to topics such as racism, colonialism and capitalism.

## THE LINGUISTIC IS POLITICAL

Over time, the political status of the peoples and nations where most of the world's linguistic diversity resides has led me to think about languages spoken in communities that don't comprise nation states and that have suffered – still suffer – from systemic colonialism: these being the only two characteristics shared by the so-called Indigenous languages of the world. The role of nation states and their homogenising project is directly related to the accelerated death of languages today, and in this context the linguistic becomes deeply political. Languages championed by nation states have a different political and social status from languages that modern nation states have historically sought to suppress. Beyond numbers of speakers, this different political status of human languages around the world has become crucial to the conversation about their vitality.

## LANGUAGE AS TERRITORY

If the linguistic is political, then it seems impossible to continue the fight for the existence of at-risk languages as though those languages were just another folkloric aspect of Indigenous peoples' cultures; rather, they should be approached as a cognitive territory which, just like Indigenous peoples' physical territories, have become spaces of dispute and resistance. I see the defence of language and the defence of territory as profoundly interlinked projects. The Mexican state, like many nation-states around the world, has historically used linguistic displacement as a tool in its project of disappearing Indigenous peoples through forced integration; in this context, the defence of language becomes strategic. Beyond celebrating diversity, it becomes necessary to put the fight for languages front and centre in processes of resisting racism and colonialism. Just as extractivist megaprojects imperil our geographical territories, the nation state's linguistic practices and customs displace us from our linguistic territories.

And so, in this way, a return visit to old texts has thrown current concerns into relief and put them in conversation with earlier reflections. The generous curation, editing, translation and publication of these texts, now in English, will allow me to share ideas and words, to talk (which I so love to do) to other people coming to this book, and through these interactions to continue to build ideas and processes in a collaborative way. Tyoskujuyëp, amuum tu'uk joojt.

28 August, 2023

# So I idealise everything, do I?

Well, what other
way is there
to inhabit this
world?

# Note on the Translation

It seems fitting for a collection of essays that regularly and enthusiastically invites participation from its readers to be framed by so many prefatory and reflective texts. The author's self-effacement ('it's a bit strange talking about myself', she says, refreshingly) and enthusiasm for collaboration means this book was always going to integrate the efforts of multiple people, not least the four editors who curated its contents for Almadía's Spanish language edition. I'm pleased to have had the opportunity to add my voice, through translation, to those who were already here.

The role played by Spanish in Mexico – its prestige, its ubiquity in the written landscape, the way it has been wielded in efforts to suppress and oppress – is roundly eclipsed by the role of English globally. What's more, as Gitanjali Patel and Nariman Youssef recently pointed out in an essay for *Asymptote*, 'the work of Anglophone translators – venturing out, bringing back, understanding the other by making them in their image' too often follows 'the routes of colonial acquisition' ('All the Violence It May Carry on its Back', 2021). Though this new English language edition cannot help but contribute to the overwhelming excess of English in the global written landscape, I have endeavoured to understand

and 'remake' this book on its own terms. To emulate the author's loose, chatty style, the intimacy, familiarity and generosity with which she writes, and which belies her enormous erudition.

A few translational decisions are worth mentioning. First, I have included Yásnaya's social media posts written in Mixe without translating them into English. I hope that their appearance in this volume will spur readers to make that 'powerful gesture of respect': to do some research and learn enough to decipher them of their own accord. To swim in that 'sonorous sea', as Yásnaya puts it, and watch the islands of meaning grow. Everything that I have translated has been translated from Spanish, even where it was a previous translation from Mixe or another language.

Second, departing from the Spanish edition, I have included all 'non-English' words in regular font rather than italics. Khairani Barokka articulates the motivation for this decision particularly eloquently when she describes the practice of italicising such words as 'a form of linguistic gatekeeping' that marks a boundary between words that are 'exotic', 'other', or 'foreign' and those that have a rightful place in an English language text ('The Case Against Italicizing Foreign Words', *Catapult*, 11 Feb, 2020). In the Almadía edition of this book, Mixe words always appear in italics, even the transcription of an entire Mixe speech ('Nëwemp, ja nëëj jets ja ää ayuujk', pp. 203–207); this seems to me to go against the spirit of Yásnaya's writing. There is nothing foreign about Mixe or any of Mexico's many other languages in the cultural contexts this book discusses, so I see no reason to estrange them visually, quite the opposite – to do so is to reinforce Hispanophone (or, in the case of this edition, Anglophone) cultural dominance. Barokka also points out that the decision to italicise or not is a question of assumed audience. If I italicise a Mixe word, I assume a lack of familiarity with it, and so risk alienating any reader – one of the many California-resident migrants from Oaxaca, say – who does have knowledge of that language, and for whom we might anticipate this book to have special relevance and resonance.

Third, I've made the perhaps unusual choice to translate 'pueblos originarios' as 'original peoples' and 'lenguas originarias' as 'original languages'. This avoids eliding them with 'pueblos indígenas' ('Indigenous peoples') and 'lenguas indígenas' ('Indigenous languages') where Yásnaya moves back and forth between these terms, as well as the sometimes negative connotations of the word 'native'.

Finally, I've capitalised the words 'Indigenous' and 'Black', as is now customary in some parts of the English-speaking world as a sign of respect for the political and historical communities they denote (in the same way that the terms 'German' or 'Asian' are capitalised), even though it is not currently the convention to capitalise 'negro' or 'indígena' in Spanish.

It only remains to say (with a little help from a friend): Yásnaya, tyoskujuyëp ku ëts xkupiky yïn äw ayuujk.

**Ellen Jones**
Mexico City, 2023

CHARCO PRESS

Director & Editor: Carolina Orloff
Director: Samuel McDowell

www.charcopress.com

*This Mouth is Mine* was published on
70gsm Enso paper.

The text was designed using Bembo 11.5 and ITC Galliard.

Printed in May 2024 by TJ Books
Padstow, Cornwall, PL28 8RW using responsibly
sourced paper and environmentally-friendly adhesive.

MIX
Paper from
responsible sources
FSC® C013056